Sea
Disasters

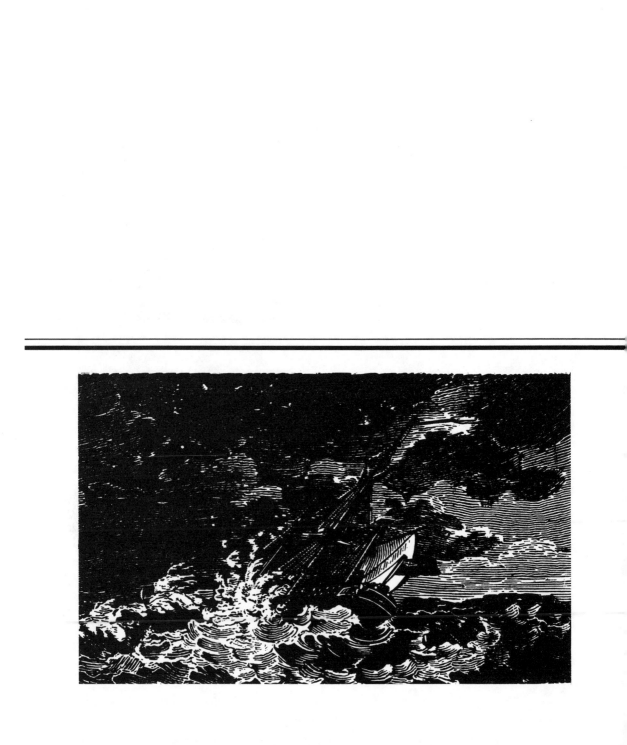

Sea
Disasters

WALTER R. BROWN
AND
NORMAN D. ANDERSON

 ADDISON-WESLEY

Text Copyright © 1981 by Walter R. Brown and Norman D. Anderson
Illustrations Copyright © 1981 by Addison-Wesley Publishing Company, Inc.
All Rights Reserved
Addison-Wesley Publishing Company, Inc.
Reading, Massachusetts 01867
Printed in the United States of America

ABCDEFGHIJK-DO-8987654321

Library of Congress Cataloging in Publication Data

Brown, Walter R
     Sea disasters.

          Includes index.
          SUMMARY: Accounts of eight disasters, including the attack of the Essex
by a whale in 1820 and the sinking of the Titanic in 1912 and of the submarine
Thresher in 1963.
          1. Shipwrecks—Juvenile literature. [1. Shipwrecks]
I. Anderson, Norman D., joint author. II. Title.
G525.B858   363.1'23'09   80-27156
ISBN 0-201-09154-2

Contents

Attack by a Whale

CHAPTER ONE

November, 1820 found the whaleship *Essex* sailing the Pacific Ocean nearly 2,500 miles west of Ecuador, South America. She was a small ship— only 105 feet long. But she and her crew of 20 had sailed all the way from Nantucket, an island off the coast of Massachusetts. Home for these sailors was almost on the other side of the world.

Voyages such as this one were not unusual for whalemen of Nantucket. Their trips often lasted two years and sometimes even longer. But their long voyages were usually worth the effort and hardship. With a good catch, they would return home rich men.

They were not hunting just ordinary whales. They sailed the unknown Pacific in search of the huge, dangerous sperm whale. From these monstrous

animals, the men took oil. This whale oil was sold as fuel for the lamps that were used to light homes in those days. The oil of the sperm whale burned with a brighter light than the oil from other whales. Because of this, sperm oil brought a higher price. But even more valuable was a waxy material the men found in the whale skull. It was called *spermaceti* and was used to make candles and a healing salve. Spermaceti was actually worth its weight in silver!

The *Essex* had left Nantucket Island on August 12, 1819. The oldest man on board was 29-year-old Captain George Pollard, Jr. The youngest on the crew was a 15-year-old cabin boy named Thomas Nickerson.

The ship had sailed down the east coast of North and South America. On the way two stops were made to buy vegetables and some live pigs. The *Essex* reached the tip of South America just before Christmas. As the little ship rounded Cape Horn, she met strong winds that blew straight out of the west. She battled these cold winds for five weeks before finally rounding the Cape and entering the Pacific Ocean.

Once clear of the Cape, Captain Pollard turned the *Essex* north and into the whale hunting grounds. As they sailed up the coast of South America the crew killed whale after whale. By the end of the summer of 1820, the men had collected nearly 1000 barrels of oil.

They spent most of the month of October on the Galapagos Islands. These islands lie on the equator just west of Ecuador. Here the crew rested and caught 360 of the huge turtles that have made these islands

Crew of the *Essex* on the
Galapagos Islands catching
turtles for food.

famous. The turtles were to be used as fresh food on the rest of the voyage. So far, the trip had been easy and profitable.

But trouble began with the first attack on a whale after the *Essex* left the Galapagos Islands. It was on the 16th of November. A group of whales (called a *shoal*) was sighted and three of the 28-foot-long whaleboats were lowered into the water. Captain Pollard was in charge of one whaleboat. First Mate Owen Chase commanded another. Matthew Jay, the Second Mate, directed the crew of the third boat.

Owen Chase, the First Mate, was 23. This was only his second trip to the Pacific in search of sperm whales. However, he was an expert with the hand-thrown harpoon, and it was his job to make the first strike. He stood in the bow of the whaleboat, legs braced, harpoon ready, waiting for the whale to surface. Suddenly the whale struck at the tiny boat with its huge tail. Chase and his crew were thrown into the water. When they looked around, they found their whaleboat was rapidly sinking.

The other whaleboats soon picked them up. Much to everyone's surprise, no one had been seriously injured by the incident. But a valuable boat had been lost.

Four days later, on November 20, another shoal of whales was spotted. Again three whaleboats were put into the water. And again, Chase stood in the bow, waiting for the monster that lay below them. Suddenly there it was, just a few yards ahead. Quickly the men rowed their whaleboat forward. Chase leaned forward and plunged the sharp harpoon deeply into the whale's back.

The whale thrashed back and forth with its tail. And again the boat was smashed by the huge tail. Owen Chase quickly cut the rope that tied the boat to the harpoon. He then ordered the crew to row the boat away from the thrashing whale. Chase stuffed his shirt into the broken side of the whaleboat, and the crew rowed back to the *Essex*.

The damaged boat was quickly lifted from the water and turned upside down on the deck of the ship. The hole was not large. Chase began to make temporary repairs to the whaleboat with a sheet of canvas. Suddenly the First Mate saw the largest sperm whale he had ever seen. The huge animal had surfaced and was lying quietly in the water about 100

A harpooned whale lifts a whaleboat out of the sea and throws it over with its great tail.

7

yards away. At the time, Chase estimated that the whale was only a bit shorter than the *Essex* itself.

Work on the deck of the *Essex* stopped, and the men watched the strange sight. The whale floated quietly and seemed to be watching the ship. Then the whale spouted two or three times and slowly sank out of sight. The men on the *Essex* relaxed and talked excitedly about the thing they had just seen. Then the whale suddenly appeared again. This time it was less than 100 feet away. And it was moving rapidly — *directly toward the ship!*

At the time the *Essex* was under part sail. The whaleship was moving at about three miles an hour. Chase estimated that the whale was moving at about the same speed and was headed directly for the bow of the ship. Before anyone could make a move to turn the ship, the whale struck with a tremendous crash. The *Essex* shuddered and trembled as if she had struck a rock.

The whale passed under the ship and surfaced. For a few minutes the animal thrashed around in the water. Then the huge beast sank out of sight.

Owen Chase ordered the pumps started, just in case the crash had damaged the ship. But before this could be done, one of the crew shouted a warning.

"There it is! It's making for us again!"

Amazed, Chase and the other men rushed to the bow of the ship. Sure enough, nearly a half mile dead ahead was the whale. This time it was moving very rapidly, perhaps twice as fast as before. The *Essex* was still sailing before the wind and, as before, took the blow nearly head-on.

The First Mate knew that the ship had been badly damaged by the attack. He quickly gave orders to the men. The only undamaged boat was quickly launched. Navigation equipment and maps were brought from the Captain's cabin. Food and clothing were thrown into the waiting boat. Then the men tumbled to safety as the *Essex* slowly rolled over on her side.

The other two whaleboats, returning from their whale searches, soon joined the survivors. You can imagine the surprise of the men in them when they heard what had happened.

Captain Pollard quickly took charge of the situation. The *Essex* lay on her side, slowly sinking into the sea. Pollard ordered two boats to get as close to the sinking ship as possible. The men in them began to pick up anything that floated free from the wreck. Meanwhile, Captain Pollard took his boat to the masts and cut loose as much of the sail as he could.

Owen Chase led some of his crew onto the side of the sinking ship. The men quickly cut through the side and into the food storage lockers. Through this hole they were able to pull fresh water, bread, guns, a few turtles, and a tool box.

The *Essex* struggled against the waves and wind for another two days. Her crew had taken everything they could find from her. On November 22, the *Essex* finally broke apart and sank. The three whaleboats and their 20 passengers were alone on an empty ocean, hundreds of miles from the nearest land.

The Galapagos Islands lay 1,500 miles to the east. But, because of the wind's direction, Captain

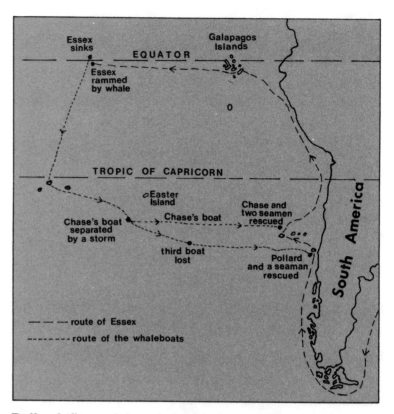

Pollard figured it would be impossible for them to travel in that direction. So he decided to allow the wind to carry them south. He hoped that they could sail to the Tropic of Capricorn. There they would probably find a west wind to take them back to the coast of South America.

During the next few days, the wind pushed them steadily southward. For this they were thankful. But the wind soon grew in strength and they were forced to take in their ragged sails. Waves often broke over the low sides of the boats. The storm made life aboard the small boats unpleasant and also ruined some of the food the men had been able to save.

On the sixth day after leaving the wreck of the *Essex*, the wind began to blow from the south. During the next few days they drifted back toward the equator. On the last day of November, Captain Pollard figured that they were less than 500 miles south of where the *Essex* had sunk. The wind again began to blow from the north. The three whaleboats were again making good progress.

Drinking water, however, had become a serious problem. The Captain and the Mates had decided to give each person only a small ration of water each day. By day the tropic sun burned down on them. Only a little shade was thrown by the sails. A sudden rainstorm struck them on December 8. But their attempts to use some fresh rainwater caught in the sails did not work. The sails had soaked up too much sea water. The rainwater quickly became salty from the sails.

Two days later the men killed and ate the last of the turtles they had managed to get from the *Essex*. The supply of bread was running low. The water was almost gone. Hunger and thirst were always with them. And, worst of all, each of the three boats had developed several leaks. In spite of the heat, the men had to work steadily to keep the water bailed out.

Five days before Christmas, land was sighted. This was exactly a month after the huge whale had attacked the *Essex*. Land turned out to be a deserted island about six miles long and three miles wide. It is easy to imagine how relieved the men were to be back on firm ground at last!

On the island, the men of the *Essex* found many birds. The men were able to catch them easily, since the birds had never seen people before. The eggs found in some of the nests also were gladly eaten.

Several good-tasting plants were found. And, after two days of searching, they found a spring of fresh water. For the first time in over a month, the men slept with full stomachs.

At first, the men thought they should stay on the tiny island until a ship came to rescue them. However, by Christmas Day, they discovered that it was becoming harder and harder to find enough food for all 20 of them. So the decision was made to repair the boats as best they could and again push out to sea. Three of the men decided to stay behind. So only 17 men were in the three boats when they left on December 27.

The birds and other food they brought with them from the island lasted for only a week. The three whaleboats were now south of the Tropic of Capricorn. The men wanted to sail east to the coast of South America or to one of the islands that lay between them and the coast. However, the winds blew them farther and farther south.

On the 8th of January, 1821, the first man died. Second Mate Matthew Joy had suffered the most during the six weeks in the open boat. Two days later he was buried at sea. The next afternoon, a new storm smashed across the open ocean. In the rain, the tossing sea, and the darkness of the night, the boats became separated. The morning found First Mate Owen Chase and his crew drifting alone in the open ocean. Captain Pollard's boat, containing five men, and the other whaleboat, carrying six men, had been blown far to the south.

The next month was one day of suffering followed by another for the men in the three tiny boats.

A typical American whaling ship.

The burning hot sun beat down on them. Their food ration was cut to a slice and a half of bread a day. On January 20, another man in Owen Chase's boat died of starvation and exposure. By this time, no one was strong enough to sail the boats. The boats drifted wherever the wind took them.

By the 8th of February, the crew of Owen Chase's boat knew it was doomed. One of the crew, a man named Isaac Cole, died after many hours of suffering. His hunger and the glaring sun drove him

13

completely insane as he thrashed around the boat in his pain. The next morning, the three men who were left were getting ready to bury their friend in the sea. Owen Chase, however, had another idea. Their food supply was down to a small handful of bread. He knew that it would all be gone within three days. After that, they were all sure to die. The only way to survive, he told his men, was to eat the dead man's body!

The men in the other two boats had reached the same conclusion nearly a month earlier. Their food supply had been completely used by January 14. Four men — Lawson Thomas, Charles Shorter, Isaiah Shepherd, and Samuel Reed — died. Their bodies had been eaten during the next two weeks.

Then, as Captain Pollard's boat and the one accompanying him drifted through the dark night of January 28, they became separated. Captain Pollard's boat survived the night but the other boat and the three men in it were never seen again.

By February 15, the three men left in Owen Chase's boat were without food again. Thomas Nickerson, the 15-year-old cabin boy, told his friends goodbye. He crawled under a sail to wait to die. But, as the boy did this, Owen Chase spotted the sail of the English ship *Indian*. Within hours, the three survivors were safely aboard.

The four men in Captain Pollard's whaleboat were also out of food. On the 1st of February, they had drawn lots to see which of them had to die so the others could live. Owen Coffin drew the short straw and was immediately shot to death. On the 11th, one of the three remaining men died from exposure. The two remaining men in Captain Pollard's boat managed to stay alive until February 23, when the American whaleship *Dauphin* found them.

Only five men survived the long voyage in the tiny boats. They had sailed more than 3500 miles in three months.

The three men who had been left on the island were found alive nearly two months later. All eight returned to their families on Nantucket Island. No one on the island questioned the fact that they had eaten their shipmates, or even that one had been murdered. They all understood how terrible it was to be adrift on the open sea in a small whaleboat.

All eight men returned to the sea. Captain Pollard took command of the whaleship *Two Brothers* and was again shipwrecked in the Pacific while hunting sperm whales. This time he and his crew were picked up after only two days of drifting in their whaleboats. But that was enough for Pollard. He never went to sea again.

Owen Chase became captain of the whaleship *Charles Carroll*. He made two successful trips to the Pacific in search of sperm whales, but soon quit the sea because of poor health. He lived the rest of his life constantly haunted by fear of starvation. When he died in 1869, the attic of his house was found to be stuffed full of food.

"Women and Children First"

CHAPTER TWO

First came the explosion in the engine room. Within minutes the British troopship *Empire Windrush* was on fire. Then, seconds later, the 1,515 men, women, and children on board were told to abandon ship. As the passengers arrived on the decks, the Commander of the troops gave orders through a megaphone.

"This is a *Birkenhead* Drill! Stand fast until you are assigned to a boat."

The soldiers formed ranks on the smoky upper decks of the sinking ship. Their families waited nearby until the order came.

"Women and children first! Into the boats!"

As the lifeboats filled with women and children were being lowered, a second order was given.

"Sick and wounded! Into the boats!"

Wreck of the steam frigate *Birkenhead* off Point Danger. Of 630 passengers and crew, 438 were lost.

During all this time the soldiers stood at attention, in spite of the smoke and heat on the deck. Officers moved up and down the ranks, picking the youngest soldiers to be ordered into the remaining lifeboats. As the last of the boats pulled away, there were still 300 soldiers standing at attention on the sinking ship. These men were ordered to jump into the water but were told to swim *away* from the lifeboats.

An hour later, a freighter arrived on the scene and picked up the survivors of the *Empire Windrush*. It was found that the only people to die in the disaster were four men killed when the boiler exploded. Some people said that the "*Birkenhead* Drill" had saved 1,511 lives on that day in March 1954.

Perhaps you have never heard of the "Birkenhead Drill." The story behind the term is an interesting one and explains why "women and children first" is one of the traditions of life at sea.

In the middle of the nineteenth century, more than 100 years ago, Victoria was Queen of Great Britian. Her empire was spread around the world. British soldiers and ships were always busy protecting their country's interests in Canada, Australia, India, and many parts of Africa.

One of the most troublesome spots in the British Empire was South Africa. Here the British troops under the command of Sir Harry Smith were at war. The native Kaffirs were trying very hard to throw the British out of their country. The war was not going well for the British and Smith had asked England for reinforcements.

Getting battle-ready troops from England to the southern tip of Africa was a difficult and dangerous job. The task was given to the HMS *Birkenhead*. The seven-year-old troopship was the Royal Navy's first iron-hulled, paddle-wheel steamer. She weighed 1,400 tons and was rigged with sails, as were most steamboats in those days. The *Birkenhead* was the fastest, safest, most comfortable transport in the Royal Navy. Her regular crew, which included a group of Royal Marines, totaled 130 men. On this trip she was under the command of Captain Robert Salmond.

The *Birkenhead* left England on January 2, 1852. By mid-February, she rounded the tip of Africa and made her way into Simonstown. She lay in the harbor here for several days, taking on food and coal and waiting for final orders. On board were 638 people. In addition to the crew, there were 478 soldiers heading for the war. They were commanded by 37-year-old Colonel Sidney Seton. Also among the passengers were 30 women and children, most of whom were families of some of the soldiers.

Finally, on February 25, the orders arrived. The *Birkenhead* was to sail at once for Aloga Bay. The troops were badly needed, and so Captain Salmond was ordered to keep his ship as close to shore as possible in order to save time. He was also told to travel at his ship's top speed.

The weather was good and the sea calm as the *Birkenhead* drove south-southeast at nearly nine miles an hour—top speed for a paddle-wheel steamer in those days. Captain Salmond kept the ship within sight of the shore at all times. Because the ship was close to land, a man was sent to the bow of the ship. His job was "to take soundings"—that is to measure the depth of the water under the ship with a weighted line. Such a line is marked off in six-foot sections and each section is called a fathom.

The hot, sultry day finally came to an end. The crowded ship settled down for the night. Captain Salmond turned the ship over to the Officer of the Watch and went to bed. A seaman named Able Stone was sent forward to take the soundings.

At a few minutes before two in the morning, the *Birkenhead* was off of Danger Point. Able Stone, the sailor in the bow, threw his line overboard and reported the depth as being between 12 and 13 fathoms—more than 70 feet. He pulled in the line

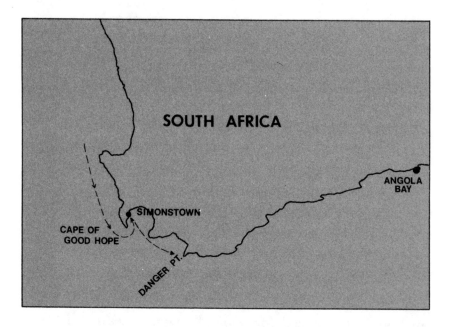

and coiled it for another sounding. But before he could throw the line, the ship smashed into an underwater rock.

The jagged rock cut through the iron bow of the ship only twelve feet below the water line. Tons of water poured into the compartments where the soldiers slept. Many of them drowned in their hammocks. The survivors rushed to the decks above. However, there was no panic or confusion. No one shouted or cried. These were soldiers of the British Army and they were proud of their discipline. They quickly formed ranks and stood at attention, waiting for orders.

Captain Salmond quickly took control of his stricken ship. The engines were stopped, a small anchor was dropped, lifeboats were uncovered, and pumps were started. Below, the water level in the engine room was rising at a rate of three or four feet per minute. The boiler fires were quickly drowned. The engineer ordered his men to the upper decks and closed the engine room doors tightly behind him. After hearing the engineer's report, Captain Salmond knew that his ship could not be saved.

Fifty soldiers were called from the ranks to man the pumps. Seven were sent to get the horses overboard. Sixty more were ordered to try to clear the wreckage from the boat deck. The rest of the troops stood silently at attention on the now slanting deck. The men were so quiet that orders could be heard as easily as if they had been on a parade ground. The men could even hear the hiss of rockets being launched from the bow to tell passing ships of the disaster.

Then came the report that most of the boats could not be launched. Several had been crushed by wreckage that had fallen on them. Others were wedged into their davits, the small cranes used to raise and lower the lifeboats. Broken ropes kept others from being put into the water. Only three small boats were found to be usable. Captain Salmond and Colonel Seton decided that the women and children were to be placed in these three boats. The only men allowed to leave were the crews needed to get the boats to shore. As the boats were loaded, the soldiers continued to stand quietly at attention.

Just as the three lifeboats pulled away, the *Birkenhead* began to break apart. The bow and foremast broke loose, jumped forward, and sank immediately. The funnel stack crashed down, crushing some of the men who were working to free more boats. Water rushed in and over the men working at the pumps. Still the troops on the deck kept their straight ranks.

It was apparent to everyone on board that the ship could not be saved. She settled quickly by the bow. The *Birkenhead* was rapidly filling with water. As the stern rose, Captain Salmond shouted, "All those who can swim, jump overboard and make for the boats!"

Colonel Seton looked at the three small boats, already crowded with women and children. Several hundred soldiers and marines had survived so far and stood waiting his orders. If they all tried to reach the safety of the three boats, they would certainly swamp or capsize the tiny craft.

"Stand fast!" he ordered his men. "No man is to go over the side!"

The lines straightened. Shoulders stiffened. Chins were pulled in. Eyes stared straight ahead. It was hard to keep a footing as the hulk rolled heavily. Still, not a single man broke the ranks.

What was left of the *Birkenhead* broke apart again as her stern lifted clear of the water. Only then did the lines of soldiers break. The sea was suddenly full of struggling men and sharks.

Troops awaiting orders on the deck of the *Birkenhead* while women and children are put into lifeboats.

Colonel Seton, who could not swim, drowned almost immediately. Captain Salmond swam strongly toward shore, then suddenly disappeared as a shark struck him from below. Others died when they became tangled in wreckage or seaweed.

But a few managed to drift ashore on the larger pieces of wreckage. Thirty or so men hung onto the masts of the sunken ship until morning. Shortly after daybreak they were rescued by the schooner *Lioness*.

Of the 638 people on board the *Birkenhead*, only 193 reached shore. Among these were all of the women and children that had been on the ship. They were alive because of the heroic action of the British soldiers and marines.

The courage of these soldiers and marines was described in a poem by Rudyard Kipling. Queen Victoria dedicated a memorial to them. And the King of Prussia was so impressed that he ordered their story read to all his soldiers.

But most important, the action of the brave men on the *Birkenhead* set an example that has become a tradition. When disaster strikes, the strong have a responsibility to see that others are safe before trying to save themselves. This is what is meant by the famous cry, "Women and children first!"

"God Himself Could Not Sink This Ship"

CHAPTER THREE

L ifeboats?" Mrs. Astor's voice showed surprise. "I thought the *Titanic* was supposed to be unsinkable."

First Officer William Murdock had just led Colonel and Mrs. John Jacob Astor on a brief tour of the first class section of the huge ship. He had met them as they boarded the passenger liner. They had then taken a quick look at the first class dining room in the middle of D Deck. An elevator had carried them to the boat deck, where they now stood.

"She is unsinkable, Madam." First Officer Murdock let his hand brush lightly against one of the sixteen lifeboats that lined the deck. "The *Titanic* is the world's largest and safest ship."

"He is correct, Mrs. Astor. God Himself could not sink this ship."

Lifeboats, filled with survivors, are rowed away from the sinking ship. There were only 16 lifeboats for the more than 2200 people on board.

At the sound of the deep voice, the couple turned. Here was the man they had come to the boat deck to meet. Mrs. Astor looked him over carefully as her husband introduced them.

Captain Edward L. Smith looked like the captain of a huge passenger liner. He was nearly sixty, and his heavy beard and mustache were flecked deeply with gray. He was not very tall, but he was slim. He wore a dress-white uniform. The brim of his cap, that he touched as he bowed slightly to his wealthy guests, was trimmed with gold braid.

"I thought you were due to retire, Captain," Astor said.

"I was. But as Senior Captain of the White Steamship Line, I put it off for just one more trip. I feel it is my duty to take the company's new ships out

27

on their first voyage. Besides, I wouldn't want to miss this historic trip. The design of this ship will be a model for shipbuilding for years to come!"

"I've seen the plans," Astor said. "Is she really unsinkable?" Colonel Astor was interested in ship design. He was a builder and inventor, as well as being one of the world's wealthiest men.

"She is as nearly unsinkable as can be built. She has two hulls, one inside the other." The Captain led them inside the wheelhouse at the front of the boat deck. It was from here that the ship was steered.

"Fifteen thick, steel walls divide the lower deck into 16 compartments," he explained to Mrs. Astor. "At the push of this button," he continued, pointing to a red button near the wheel, "electric motors close and seal steel doors. That makes each compartment completely watertight.

"The engineers who designed the ship figure that the worst that could happen to her would be a collision with another ship. An accident like that might puncture both hulls and flood the compartment inside. There is a slight chance, of course, that such a hole might be made at the point where a crosswall joins the hulls. If that happened, *two* compartments might flood. The engineers' figures show that the ship will float easily with two compartments flooded. She would even survive with as many as three compartments filled with water. A worse accident than that is impossible."

He shook hands again with Astor and again welcomed the two aboard the *Titanic*. As he watched them leave, he saw Murdock again brush his hand lightly against one of the lifeboats. Neither of the men had mentioned to their passengers that the *Titanic* carried only enough lifeboats for about half of the people on board.

As they made their way to their staterooms, Colonel Astor and the First Officer told Mrs. Astor more about the great ship.

"From the lowest point of the keel to the top of the four funnels is 175 feet," Astor told his wife. "The boat deck is more than 60 feet above the water line."

"Do you know the tallest building in New York City?" Murdock asked.

Mrs. Astor laughed. "My husband *owns* the tallest building in New York," she said.

Murdock was embarrassed. He would rather be steering the huge ship than trying to be polite to multi-millionaires. He had forgotten that Colonel Astor was the great-grandson of the first John Jacob Astor—the man who had bought farmland 100 years ago and who turned that land into vast riches as New York City grew.

"The *Titanic* is nearly twice as long as that building is tall," he mumbled. "There are over 1,300 passengers on board and we have a crew of 898."

Murdock left the Astors in their staterooms with the steward who would serve them during the trip. The rooms were large, with dark paneling and thick carpets. The beds were draped with heavy red velvet.

Two decks below them, on D Deck, a young science teacher named Lawrence Beesley had found his cabin, too. It was just a single room with a narrow bunk and no windows. But it suited him just fine. He opened one of his suitcases and began piling books from it onto a small table.

Across the narrow corridor, the Collyer family also unpacked for the week-long trip to America. The Collyers were British citizens, but they had bought a fruit farm in Fayette Valley, Idaho. This trip was, they thought, the beginning of a great adventure for the three of them.

Below them were the tiny, cramped cabins and two large rooms lined with open bunks. This was where the third class passengers would live during the trip, and it was the most uncomfortable part of the ship. G Deck was just at the water line and right above the engine rooms.

The tiny bunks were being filled with the belongings of immigrants, leaving their homes for what they hoped would be better opportunities in the United States. One of these was an Irish girl by the name of Katherine Gilnagh.

The *Titanic* left Southhampton, England, at noon on Wednesday, April 10, 1912. The first part of the voyage went well. Sunday, April 14, found the *Titanic* in the middle of the North Atlantic. After church services, most of the passengers read, played card games or squash, wrote letters, or worked-out in the gym. Only a few tried to walk the open decks. The air was quite chilly and, as the sun went down, the temperature dropped to near freezing.

The ship's two radio operators were too busy to relax and enjoy the trip. Their radio shack was a jumble of batteries, wires, and keys. They were proud to be in charge of the most modern wireless telegraph equipment in the world. By tapping out Morse Code on their key, they could send messages hundreds of miles across the ocean. The passengers had asked that dozens and dozens of messages be sent ahead to New York.

Messages came to the *Titanic*'s radio room from other ships, too. Several of these told of icebergs and sheets of ice in the water near the course of the big liner. These warnings were written out and taken to the wheelhouse. At 9:25 in the evening, Captain Smith gave the ice warnings to the officer in charge and went to bed. According to the messages from other ships, the *Titanic* would not reach the danger area for several hours.

Fifteen minutes later, a radio message was received warning of "icebergs and pack ice" between Latitude 42° N to 41°25' N; Longitude 49° to 50°30' W. Radio Operator John Phillips was busy trying to get the passengers' messages out. He wrote the location of the ice on a scrap of paper, but did not bother to take it to the wheelhouse. He did not realize that the *Titanic* had just entered the area described in the radio message.

At 10 p.m. First Officer William Murdoch took over command of the ship. He was given the old warnings about ice ahead. He passed these on to the two men on watch in the crow's nest, high above the ship's boat deck. Seamen Fleet and Lee reported that they could see fairly well in spite of there being no moon, since the stars were shining brightly. They told Murdoch that from where they were the sea was so calm it looked "slick." Murdoch replied, "I would be happier if there were a little wind." Ice lying in the

water would be easier to see if the wind were pushing waves against it.

Radio Operator Phillips stayed busy sending messages ahead to New York. Suddenly, his headphone crackled with a signal so strong it hurt his ears. It was a steamer named *California* calling. "We are stopped and surrounded by ice," the message said.

Phillips was the type of person who liked to do his job well. But he was not able to think very carefully about a new situation. He felt that he had to get the messages off to New York for the important passengers on board the *Titanic*. The loudness of the signal from the *California* should have warned him that the steamer was nearby and that the *Titanic* was heading for the ice field that surrounded the other ship. Instead, he radioed back, "Shut up! Shut up! I'm busy!" and pulled the headphones from his ears.

From the wheelhouse, Murdoch watched the water ahead carefully. He ordered a hatch cover closed because the light bothered his eyes. High above him, Fleet and Lee searched the night quietly. At 11:40, Fleet saw something in the water ahead. He pulled the alarm chain three times and yelled into the telephone. "ICEBERG—RIGHT AHEAD!"

Murdoch acted instantly. He ordered a quick turn to the left and reached for the engine room telegraph. FULL STOP, he signaled to the engine room. Then FULL REVERSE.

For half a minute, that seemed like hours, the men watched as they rushed through the darkness. As they neared it, the iceberg seemed to grow and grow until it towered above the boat deck.

CALIFORNIA
10 MILES AWAY

ICEBERG   TITANIC

NEW YORK

The ship had begun to change direction and slow down a little as she slipped past the iceberg. In their first class staterooms, Mrs. Astor heard a funny rumbling noise. She sat up in bed. Colonel Astor slept through the crash.

"Wake up, John," she said. "Something's happened. Perhaps there was an explosion in the kitchen. Go see if there is a fire."

Colonel Astor got up, pulled a silk robe over his pajamas, and went out on deck.

In the second class section of D Deck, eight-year-old Marjory Collyer also slept through the funny rumbling noise. Both of her parents were still awake and felt the slight jolt. Mrs. Collyer had an up-

The *Titanic* received a fatal gash
below the waterline when she
struck the iceberg.

set stomach and stayed in bed while Harvey Collyer stepped out into the corridor. There he met Laurence Beesley.

"I say! Did you feel that crash?" Harvey Collyer asked.

"No," the science teacher answered. "I was lying on my bunk reading. I could feel the motion of the boat and it had almost rocked me to sleep. Then, suddenly, I couldn't feel the rhythm of the ship's movement anymore. I think we have stopped."

"Let's go up and investigate, shall we?" Collyer suggested.

In the dining rooms, the stewards' talking was interrupted by the rattling of the dishes and silverware they had put in place for breakfast. The baker swore as a pan of rolls he had just taken from the oven fell from the counter top to the deck. A card game was interrupted briefly by the sight of a mountain of glistening white ice sliding past the windows.

On the lower decks of the ship, it was a different story. The crewmen on duty in the boiler rooms had jumped into action when the signal from Murdoch arrived. As they worked, turning valves and shoveling coal, they felt a terrible shock. Coal was thrown from the bins and men were thrown off their feet.

Murdoch had felt only a slight jar as they passed the iceberg, but he knew what that shock meant. He quickly pressed the button that controlled the watertight doors. Red lights flashed and bells rang their warning throughout the 16 compartments of the lowest deck. Fifteen steel doors slid shut and sealed tightly. Just then, the sea broke through. The greenish water swirled around the pipes and machinery. Firemen, stokers, and engineers in boiler rooms 5 and 6 scrambled up safety ladders as the water rose behind them. Ahead of the boiler rooms were a baggage compartment, two cargo holds, and a chain locker. Each was sealed off by the watertight doors, but each was rapidly filling with water.

The third class passengers were only one deck above the boiler rooms and felt the shock nearly as strongly as did the crewmen below. Those in the front of the ship knew that something was terribly wrong. One of these was the Irish girl, Katherine Gilnagh. She felt that she had to get out of those cramped spaces that were so near the water. But she had no idea where she should go. There had been no boat drills and no one had told any of the passengers where the lifeboat deck was or how to get there. Katherine began to climb the stairs. All she knew was she wanted to go up.

Captain Smith had taken command of the ship from First Officer Murdoch. The ship's carpenter quickly arrived in the wheelhouse.

"She's hurt bad," he reported. "There's a gash below the water line, running from the bow to boiler room 5. We're taking water into six compartments!"

Smith, along with one of the engineers who had helped design the ship, made a quick trip below. With six compartments damaged, they decided, there was nothing they could do to save the ship.

Meanwhile, most of the passengers in the first and second class sections of the ship had returned to their rooms. Colonel Astor told his wife that they had struck an iceberg but that "it didn't look serious." Harvey Collyer told his wife the same thing. "An officer told me there's no danger," he said.

Lawrence Beesley had a different idea. He, too, had been told there was no danger and had started back to his room. As he walked down the stairway, he noticed a strange thing. The stairs "weren't quite right." They seemed level, yet his feet didn't land where he expected them to. He felt as if he were stepping too far forward on each step. Suddenly he realized what this meant. The ship was tilting forward slightly. He hurried to his cabin and put on his warmest clothing, stuffed his pockets with books, and returned to A Deck.

It was now 12:05 in the morning — 25 minutes after the iceberg had brushed the ship. Captain Smith ordered the lifeboats uncovered. Stewards were sent through the ship to tell the passengers to put on lifejackets and move to the boat deck. Radio Operator Phillips was ordered to send a call for help. Over and over he tapped the message "CQD-MGY 41°46'N; 50°14'W."

"CQD" was, in 1912, the universal call for help. The signal "SOS" that we use today had only recently been suggested because it was easier to send and to understand. Later that night, Phillips switched to the SOS signal. This was the first time this signal had been used by a ship in need of help.

The Astors took time to dress carefully. Neither of them believed that the *Titanic* could possibly be in danger. When they reached the boat deck, they went into the gymnasium and sat on a pair of mechanical exercising horses.

"We are safer here than in that little lifeboat," Colonel Astor assured his wife.

The Collyers were less concerned about how they looked. They threw a lap rug around the sleeping Marjory and carried her to the boat deck.

Katherine Gilnagh couldn't find her way to the boat deck. She had no idea where it was and found herself wandering around the now-empty corridors of B Deck.

The frantic CQD signal was heard immediately by many ships. The German steamer *Frankfort* signaled "OK" at 12:18. The Canadian ship *Mt. Temple*, the American liner *Virginian,* the Russian steamer *Birma,* and the *Titanic*'s sister ship, the *Olympia,* all heard the distress signal and changed course, heading for the crippled ship. Messages of encouragement flew through the air. But all of these ships were 150 or more miles away. It would be hours and hours before any of them reached the *Titanic*'s position.

There was a ship much closer to the damaged *Titanic.* In fact, the *California* was so close Captain Smith could see her lights. This was the ship that had warned the *Titanic* of the ice field where she still lay, just 10 miles north of the sinking ship. But no one on the *California* realized the *Titanic* was in trouble. Shortly after being told to "Shut up" by the liner's radio operator, the only radioman on the *California* had shut his equipment off and gone to bed. A signal light was used to try to get the attention of the men on the *California,* but it was not answered.

The passenger liner *Carpathia* was only 60 miles away, but she too carried only one radio operator. His name was Harold Cottom. At the time the first calls for help went out from the *Titanic,* Cottom was not at his radio. He had gone to the bridge to deliver a message and to chat over a cup of coffee with the men on watch. At 12:25, he returned to his post. Hearing the CQD signal, he tapped out the message, CARPATHIA—COMING HARD, and ran for the wheelhouse. Even at top speed, the liner was nearly four hours away.

The lights of the *California* still twinkled dimly in the distance. A man was sent to the stern of the *Titanic* to fire off signal rockets to try to attract the attention of the other ship. On board the *California,* Seaman James Gibson saw the rockets. He studied the lights of the liner through binoculars. He pointed out the rockets to Second Officer Herbert Stone. Neither man guessed that the fireworks were a last, desperate call for help.

The *Titanic* had now begun to settle heavily in its bow. The officers and crewmen were trying to get the passengers into the boats. The passengers were confused. They had not been given a boat drill and did not know what to do. The ship's crew were not even certain to which boats they had been assigned. "Women and children first!" they shouted. They tried to allow men in the boats only after as many women as possible were already in.

Some of the passengers fought to get into the boats. Others refused to leave at all. Mrs. Isidor Straud did not want to leave her husband, and he would not go until everyone else was safe. So, hand in hand, the elderly couple sat quietly in deck chairs until the water claimed them.

Lifeboat #4 had been lowered until it was level with A Deck. Windows were broken out and deck chairs were placed against the rail. Colonel Astor lifted his wife up in his arms and passed her over the windowsill and into the boat. He then leaned through the window and kissed her lightly.

"I'll see you later, Dearie," he said calmly. He then turned and walked slowly down the slanting deck.

Marjory Collyer was quickly passed to the people already in Lifeboat #14. Mrs. Collyer was ready to climb into the boat when she realized her husband was going to stay behind. "I won't go without you," she screamed.

A seaman grabbed Mrs. Collyer by the arms. Another grabbed at her waist. Together they dragged her, kicking and screaming, into the boat.

"Go, Lottie! For God's sake, be brave and go! I'll get a seat in another boat!" her husband shouted. But there were no seats in another boat for him.

Lawrence Beesley found a seat in the last boat to leave the ship. So did Katherine Gilnagh. She had found her way to A Deck, but could not find the stairs that led to the boat deck. As she ran down the slanting deck, she saw a man — the only person she had seen on the entire deck. He was standing by the railing, watching Lifeboat #4 pull away from the ship.

"Sir! Sir! Can you help me?" the crying girl pleaded. "I can't find the stairs."

Colonel Astor knew how crowded the boat deck was, and how few of these people were going to get into the last few boats. Instead of taking the girl to the stairs, he led her to the rail.

"Climb up on my shoulders," he ordered. "One of the seamen on the deck above will pull you into a lifeboat."

This was quickly done. As the lifeboat was lowered into the sea, Katherine saw the man for the last time, leaning against the rail, calmly watching the boats pull away into the night.

Engineers, firemen, and stokers worked at keeping the boilers going to give the ship the electricity it needed for the radio signals and for lights. They died at their posts, 122 feet below the boat deck.

The band leader had called his seven musicians to the boat deck. There they played happy Ragtime music as the boats were being filled. As the last boat pulled away and the water began to lap around their ankles, they began playing hymns. One by one, they slipped down the slanting deck and into the dark, cold water.

Radioman Phillips continued to tap out a steady call for help. Radioman Cottom on the *Carpathia* listened helplessly as his big liner smashed its way northward. At 2:17 the signal sputtered "CQ . . ." and stopped. The *Titanic* was gone. The *Carpathia* was still more than two hours away.

On board the *California,* only ten miles away, Seaman Gibson reported that he could no longer see lights from the liner. "She must have turned and moved farther south," he reported.

There were 16 lifeboats and two rubber liferafts in the water when the *Titanic* finally stood straight up on her bow and slipped into the ocean. The lifeboats were not completely full, but even if they had been there would not have been enough room in them for more than half of the people on board the ship.

The temperature of the water was 28°F. A person can live for only a short while in water at that temperature. When the *Carpathia* arrived two hours later, everyone who was still in the water was dead.

The rescue liner picked up a total of only 705 survivors. Nearly 1,500 people had died along with the "world's largest and safest ship."

U.S. Navy plane flying past a giant iceberg like the one the *Titanic* struck.

A memorial service for those who
were lost was held at the site of
the wreck of the *Titanic*.

Only 19 percent of the men on board the *Titanic* were saved. The others had given their places in the lifeboats to the women and children. Nearly 77 percent of the women and 50 percent of the children survived the sinking.

Twenty-three percent of the crew lived. Many of these were men who were responsible for the lifeboats. Their job was to see that the passengers in the lifeboats were taken care of. The other crew members stayed at their duty stations and died. Of the 120 engineers, firemen, and stokers who kept the boilers going until the last minute, only eight survived. All of the members of the band, all of the postal clerks, all of the cabin boys, and all of the pursers died. Captain Edward Smith also went down with his ship.

Murder at Sea

Captain Walter Schwieger of the German navy was frightened. Of course he kept this a secret from his crew on the submarine U-20.

Schwieger had been ordered to take his submarine out of port on April 24, 1915. The other three U-boats that made up the "pack" had already left for the coast of England. But the U-20 was still safely in port. Schwieger had kept her there as long as possible. His excuse was that he was not satisfied with the repairs that had been made on his submarine. But the truth was he was afraid to go into combat again.

Perhaps he had a right to be frightened. During World War I, submarines were not the huge, beautiful boats they are today. Even the German submarines, which were the best in the world in 1915, were small and unreliable. They could not dive very

deeply. They could not stay submerged for more than
a few hours. And their torpedoes often did not ex-
plode when they hit a target. During the past nine
weeks, four German U-boats had been sunk by the
British Navy. In each case, everyone on board had
been killed, including the commanders of the submarines. All four of these men had been lifelong friends
of Walter Schwieger.

Schwieger himself had narrowly escaped death
on his last voyage. The U-20 had been on patrol in
the North Sea and found an unarmed merchant ship.
Schwieger had decided to attack with his deck gun
rather than use the unreliable torpedoes. So he surfaced and ordered the ship to stop and surrender. His
plan was to let the crew get into lifeboats before he
sank the ship. But things did not go according to
plan.

German submarines of World
War I, often called U-boats.

The U-20 had surfaced ahead of and to one side of the big ship. Instead of stopping, the ship had suddenly turned directly toward the submarine and picked up speed. Schwieger had quickly ordered a crash dive to avoid being rammed. The submarine managed to get under water before the ship arrived, but the keel of the huge vessel scraped against the submarine's periscope. Water poured into the U-20 through a crack at the base of the periscope, and for a while everyone thought the submarine was doomed. Schwieger, however, managed to get his ship safely back to port. But the near-disaster had caused him to lose his nerve. He often woke up at night in a cold sweat, thinking about the icy water pouring down on him from above.

While the U-20 sat safely in port, another submarine, the U-30, was busy sinking ships off the coast of England. On April 28, she stopped the ore-carrier *Mobile*. After allowing the crew to escape, she sank the ship with gun fire. On April 30, the U-30 found the *Fulgent*. The U-boat surfaced and ordered the ship to halt. Instead, the merchant ship tried to escape. The U-30's deck gun fired a shot that made a direct hit on the ship's bridge, killing the Captain and the Quartermaster. The Second-in-Command ordered the ship stopped and the crew into the lifeboats. The Germans boarded the *Fulgent* and took the ship's papers and some food. They then sank her with explosives set against her hull. Later that afternoon, the U-30 stopped and sank two other merchant ships after letting their crews escape in lifeboats.

As this last action took place, the U-20 was just leaving her home port. The next day, May 1,

Schwieger tested his radio. The message was picked up by the British and quickly decoded. They now knew that the U-20 was on its way to relieve the U-30 off the coast of England.

During the early months of 1915, the sea war had been controlled by the Germans. The 21 U-boats that made up the German submarine fleet had sunk a total of 49 merchant ships within a few miles of the English coast. Their job was to try to stop the steady stream of ships that carried men and supplies from Canada to England and from England to the battle-fields of Europe.

This was a difficult job. The United States was not yet involved in the war between Germany and England. And the Germans did not want to do any-thing that would make the American people angry. If they did, they knew the United States might declare war against them.

The United States was trying to help England as much as it could without actually getting into the war. Guns and ammunition were being smuggled into England. Sometimes the boxes were marked with food labels. Then they were put on passenger liners that were safe from attack by German U-boats.

The German submarines usually let passenger liners enter and leave the war zone around England. They knew that many people from the United States and other neutral countries still traveled on these ships. If the U-boats killed any of these passengers, their countries might enter the war on England's side.

This is why the German U-boats usually warned ships before they attacked them. The U-boat com-

NOTICE!

TRAVELLERS intending to embark on the Atlantic voyage are reminded that a state of war exists between Germany and her allies and Great Britain and her allies; that the zone of war includes the waters adja-cent to the British Isles; that, in accordance with formal no-tice given by the Imperial Ger-man Government, vessels fly-ing the flag of Great Britain, or of any of her allies, are liable to destruction in those waters and that travellers sailing in the war zone on ships of Great Britain or her allies do so at their own risk.

IMPERIAL GERMAN EMBASSY
WASHINGTON, D. C., APRIL 22, 1915.

This ad appeared in American newspapers. It warned of the dangers of traveling by sea in 1915.

manders usually tried very hard to identify a ship, find out what she was carrying, and let the people on board escape before sinking the ship. This is what Captain Schwieger was trying to do when the U-20 had been rammed. He was determined not to make the same mistake again.

Many of the English merchant ships were being fitted with guns so they could fight back against the German submarines. Guns that could fire six-inch shells and machine guns were put on the decks of many innocent-looking cargo ships. All troop carriers were armed. Captain Schwieger knew that he had to be very careful when he attacked a ship on the surface.

Schwieger also knew that many passenger liners had been taken over by the English government and were being used as troop carriers. One of them was the *Mauretania*. She had been built to carry passengers across the Atlantic Ocean in the greatest luxury. Her sister ship, the *Lusitania,* still made the passenger run between Liverpool and New York on a regular schedule. But the *Mauretania* now lay in the harbor at Aronmouth, taking on thousands of troops and tons of ammunition for the battles across the English Channel. Where the shuffleboard court once was, there now was a battery of six-inch guns. Where deck chairs used to be, there were machine guns behind walls of sandbags. The cargo holds were being filled with guns, bullets, and shells. The staterooms were becoming crowded with young soldiers from England, Canada, Australia, and the rest of the United Kingdom, on their way to fight the Germans.

The *Mauretania,* troop-carrying sister ship to the *Lusitania.*

On the evening of May 4, the U-20 surfaced off the coast of Ireland. As darkness closed in, Captain Schwieger began a surface run down the coast. By 9 o'clock the next morning, the U-20 was in position off Fastner Light. Here the submarine could watch the ships that entered and left the narrow St. George's Channel, which leads to the large harbor at Liverpool, England.

The day was foggy. Captain Schwieger let the U-20 drift just under the surface of the water. The man on watch kept his eye glued to the eyepiece of the periscope, turning it around and around. For hours, he saw nothing. Then, suddenly, there was a ship.

She was not much of a prize for a German submarine. The *Earl of Latham* was a sailing schooner. Schwieger ordered his U-boat to the surface. Through a speaking trumpet, he ordered the crew of the *Latham* to abandon ship and bring him the schooner's papers. He then sank the vessel with hand grenades attached to her keel.

Just before dusk, the U-20 found another ship. Schwieger followed her for awhile, trying to get into a position for a safe surface attack. But before he could do so, the fog closed in and the ship escaped.

May 6 was a better day for the U-20. The fog was still very thick. The submarine lay on the surface, but the men on watch could not see more than 30 yards ahead. Suddenly, a huge ship loomed out of the fog directly ahead of them. Two shots were fired by the submarine's gun crew before the ship disappeared back into the fog.

One of the men on board the U-20 was a civilian. Before the war his job had been to guide large ships into and out of one of Europe's largest harbors. He had been on, or seen, almost all of the ships that sailed the Atlantic Ocean. On the U-20, his job was to identify any ship spotted and give Captain Schwieger information about it. This man was called the U-boat's "pilot."

The pilot had only had a brief look at the ship that had disappeared so quickly into the fog. But he recognized her immediately. She was the steamer *Candidate*. She was being used to carry supplies between England and the battle in Europe and was an ordinary merchant ship, as far as the pilot knew.

As Schwieger discussed the ship with his pilot, the fog suddenly shifted. The U-20 and the *Candidate* found themselves not more than 50 yards apart. As soon as the submarine was spotted, the crew of the cargo ship began lowering the lifeboats. Schwieger ordered some of his men to board the ship and get her papers. When they returned, they reported that they had found a six-inch gun and several machine gun nests hidden under the cargo nets that covered the decks of the ship. Only the sudden lifting of the fog, catching the crew by surprise, had saved the U-20 from a battle with the merchant ship.

Schwieger pulled his submarine back about a quarter of a mile and fired a torpedo into the *Candidate*. It exploded nicely, but the ship seemed to be undamaged. Schwieger brought the U-20 up closer and began firing shells from the deck gun into the ship. It took almost three hours to sink the *Candidate*. Schwieger went below, complaining to himself about the poor quality of the weapons he had to fight with. The U-20 slipped quietly beneath the water.

It was only two hours later that the U-20 found another victim. The pilot identified the ship as a sister ship of the one that had just been sunk. Her name was the *Centurion*. Schwieger ran alongside the ship for awhile, looking through his periscope at the nets draped around her deck. She looked like an ordinary cargo ship. But Schwieger remembered the guns on the *Candidate*. He ordered a course change and fired a torpedo into the side of the *Centurion* without any warning.

As had happened before, the explosion of the torpedo against the side of the ship seemed to do little damage. Schwieger fired a second torpedo. The ship stopped and began to list a little. The crew quickly abandoned the ship which sank in about an hour and a half.

It was nearly dusk. Schwieger ordered the submarine out to the open sea. She would spend the night there, on the surface, letting her batteries recharge. The fog was still very heavy, and Schwieger

The passenger ship *Lusitania*.

Captain Walter Schwieger

hated it. Anything could come at him out of the swirling mist, and he would be almost helpless against it. He would have liked to take the U-20 home, but he knew he could not. He had three torpedoes left and his fuel oil was only half gone. On this tour he had sunk only two large ships and the little sailing schooner. He knew that his superiors would not be happy with this record. So, reluctantly, he decided to stay on patrol just one more day.

At dawn on May 7, the U-20 was on the surface far up in the St. George's Channel. The fog, which had remained thick throughout the night, suddenly lifted a little. There, heading straight for them, was a British patrol boat!

Schwieger's men dove for the hatches as he sounded the signal for a crash dive. Silently, the submarine slipped beneath the water. It settled to the bottom and lay there without a sound. Schwieger felt sweat roll down his face and his shirt became clammy as he listened to the patrol boat's propellers cut through the water just above his head. The nightmare of water pouring in on him flashed before him again.

But the patrol boat had not seen the U-20. It kept on its course up the channel. The sounds of its engines faded away. Schwieger ordered the submarine up off the bottom and headed in the opposite direction.

At a little before noon, the U-20 rose to periscope depth. Through the scope, Captain Schwieger saw he was opposite the entrance to the Queenstown Harbor. The fog was gone and the sun shone brightly. He swiveled the periscope around and saw a terrifying sight. A huge warship, the cruiser *Juno*, was making its way toward the harbor.

Again, the U-20's engines were stopped and the submarine settled silently to the bottom. Again the men inside listened to the dreaded sound of propellers as they pushed the cruiser through the water above them. Schwieger felt certain that the pilot who stood beside him noticed the sweat that ran down his face.

"Enough of this," Schwieger decided. "We will go home!"

But Captain Schwieger was going to fire one more torpedo before he reached the safety of his home port. That torpedo was to help bring America into the war and insure the defeat of Germany.

The *Lusitania*, the world's largest and fastest passenger liner, had left Liverpool, England, on April 17, 1915. The trip to New York was uneventful. She had left New York for her return trip early on the morning of May 1. In spite of the war in Europe, she carried a full load of passengers. Some were young

men trying to get to England to volunteer to fight the Germans. Others were English families returning home. Still others were businessmen and a few were American vacationers.

The *Lusitania* in port before sailing for Europe.

The *Lusitania* carried a strange cargo. As a passenger ship, she was not supposed to carry war supplies. But in one of her forward holds were thousands of boxes marked "cheese." Each of these weighed 40 pounds. It is now believed that these boxes contained ammunition.

The *Lusitania* entered the war zone around England during the night of May 6. The fog was heavy and its Captain slowed his huge ship to about half speed. Somewhere here he was supposed to meet the cruiser *Juno* and be escorted into the berth at Liverpool. The *Lusitania* crept through the night, its fog horn calling out to the *Juno*. But the old cruiser had been ordered to return to port at Queenstown and was more than 100 miles up the St. George's Channel. No one has ever explained why this order was given. Nor do we know why the *Lusitania* was not told that her escort would not be there to meet her.

At 1:20 the next afternoon, May 7, the U-20 was off the light at Fastner, heading for home. The man on watch reported a smudge of smoke off the starboard bow. The Captain watched it closely. He wanted no more brushes with English warships.

Within a few minutes he could see the four huge funnels of a steamship, heading for the coast. He estimated that the ship was about 14 miles away and ordered the U-20 to be submerged. Once under the water, he set a course that would take him ahead of the ship. As he drew closer to the liner, he could see her clearly through his periscope.

"Four funnels with schooner rig." He described the ship to the pilot who checked quickly through his books. "Upwards of 25,000 tons. Speed about 25 knots."

"She's either the *Lusitania* or the *Mauretania*," the pilot told him. "The *Mauretania* is known to be heavily armed and is being used to carry troops."

"She must be the *Mauretania*," Schwieger exclaimed. His voice showed his excitement. What a prize! This tour would not be a failure after all!

But he had to be very careful. A ship that large would not be easy to sink with torpedoes. But the machine guns and six-inch cannons of the troop ship would make a surface attack a very dangerous job.

The U-20 had to run at top speed submerged for over an hour to get into position. When Schwieger

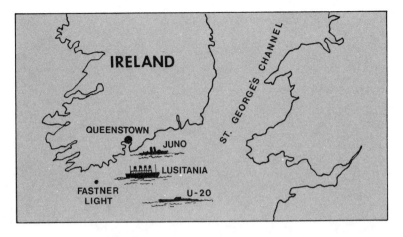

raised his periscope he found that his trap had
worked. His target had turned to follow the coast line
and was now moving directly across his bow. He
quickly ordered the range and depth setting for his
first torpedo. He waited until the huge ship was
sighted in the cross-hairs of his periscope and then ordered the torpedo fired.

The torpedo struck the *Lusitania's* side just forward of the front funnel. Schwieger, watching
through his periscope, was surprised to see a huge explosion. The first explosion was followed quickly by
an even larger one. The ship stopped immediately
and began to list badly. She also began to settle
quickly toward the bow.

Schwieger ordered the submarine to circle
around the stricken ship. Because of the bad list,
the crew was having trouble launching the lifeboats.
The big ship seemed to be ready to capsize at any
moment.

"We must have hit her ammunition hold," he
told the pilot. "She is going down fast. There is one
group of soldiers who will never reach the front!"

He was almost laughing out loud as he gave the periscope controls to the pilot. The man took one look and stepped back in shock.

"Sir!" he exclaimed. "That's not the *Mauretania!* It's the *Lusitania!* Those are civilian passengers, not soldiers!"

Grimly, Schwieger closed down the periscope and headed for home. Within 18 minutes, the *Lusitania* had disappeared beneath the water. Nearly 1,200 men, women, and children went down with her.

Among the passengers who drowned when the

The *Lusitania* sank quickly following two explosions on board after being struck by a torpedo.

Lusitania was sunk were 128 Americans. MURDER AT SEA, the newspaper headlines cried. The attitude of the people of the United States toward the war changed. Factories began to produce materials for war. Men began training to fight. And, on April 6, 1917, the United States declared war on Germany.

No one, of course, will ever really know how much Captain Schwieger's mistake had to do with the turn of events. However, if Captain Schwieger had correctly identified the *Lusitania,* the whole course of history might have been different.

The Mystery of the Cyclops

CHAPTER FIVE

The *Cyclops* was a strange ship. She looked strange. She acted differently from other ships as she moved through the water. And bad luck seemed to follow her everywhere.

The *Cyclops* had been built at the Newport News Shipbuilding and Dry Dock Company in Virginia in 1910. She was designed to carry coal and was believed to be the best designed ship of her type in the world. But she looked like no other ship. Her decks were a maze of huge booms. Twenty-four of these, 12 on each side, towered over the decks near the middle of the ship. From each boom swung a huge scoop used to lift coal into and out of the *Cyclops*'s dark, dusty holds. Almost twice as long as a football field, she carried 10,000 tons of cargo. Two propellers

drove her through the water at more than 17 miles per hour. During the eight years she was in service, she did her job well.

Only one man ever commanded the *Cyclops*. And he was even stranger than his ship. At the time World War I started, he held the rank of Lieutenant Commander in the U.S. Naval Reserves. How he became an officer is an interesting story in itself.

The records show that the captain's name was George W. Worley and that he had been born in San Francisco. But neither of these statements was true. He apparently entered the United States illegally in 1878 when he deserted from a German merchant ship. His real name was Johann Wichman, and he was born in Germany. And now, in 1918, the United

States was at war with Germany. The U.S. Navy had taken over the *Cyclops*. Worley, a German citizen, was suddenly in command of a U.S. Navy ship.

When the *Cyclops* was at sea, Captain Worley liked to walk the decks dressed only in long underwear and a derby hat. He usually had a cigar clamped tightly in his teeth and carried a cane. He often strapped a huge pistol to his side. What a strange sight he must have been!

Worley ran the *Cyclops* as if she was his empire. His decisions were law, even when they went against the judgment of his Navy superiors. Sailors breaking his rules were punished by having to run barefoot over the metal decks. When the ship was in the tropics, this punishment often caused badly burned feet. If a seaman or an officer broke what Worley thought was a more serious rule, the man was quickly put into a cell in the hold of the ship.

Worley had spent many, many years at sea, but still he was a very poor seaman. This may be why bad luck seemed always to be a passenger on the *Cyclops*.

The 260 crewmen on board hated the ship and were afraid of their Captain. Thus, it was an unhappy group of men who sailed from Norfolk, Virginia in late January, 1918. The cargo was a load of coal to be delivered to the U.S. Navy warships stationed along the east coast of South America.

There was no sun the day the ship departed. Heavy clouds covered the sky. A light snow was falling. For the first time in memory, the water of the harbor was frozen solid. As the *Cyclops* plowed through the ice, she nearly smashed into another

Navy ship. It was a bad start for a voyage. And the trip was to have an even more tragic ending.

On the fifth day out of Norfolk, Worley became angry at something First Lieutenant Forbes said. Without waiting for the man to explain, the Captain had his Second-in-Command placed under arrest.

Then, off the coast of South America, one of the ship's two engines broke down.

The harbor at Rio de Janeiro was finally reached at night. The ship's course for entering the harbor had been figured out by Lieutenant Forbes long before his arrest, but Captain Worley decided to change the plan. As the sun began to rise, the man on watch found that they were heading straight for a rocky shore. The one working engine was quickly thrown into reverse at full speed. The ship barely missed being wrecked.

Though safely inside the harbor at last, the bad luck of the *Cyclops* continued. While unloading her cargo of coal, she twice smashed into other ships. Little damage was done, but it made the crew even more nervous.

Then came the death of a seaman. He was in a small boat, checking propellers for damage. Suddenly, one of the engines turned over. The huge propeller cut into the water and the tiny boat was pulled into it. The seaman was crushed by the spinning blades and thrown into the water where he died.

One of the ships that received coal from the *Cyclops* in the harbor at Rio was the U.S.S. *Pittsburgh*. The *Pittsburgh* had been based in San Francisco when World War I broke out. Trying to avoid being drafted into the Army, a large group of tough young men had

Captain George W. Worley

joined the Navy. They were assigned to the *Pittsburgh,* where they immediately began causing trouble. During a drunken party, two of them killed a seaman with a hammer. They and the two officers who were in charge at the time were tried and found guilty of murder.

These prisoners were put on board the *Cyclops* to be returned to the United States. Some other new passengers on the coal ship were 42 men who were being sent home for reassignment. Among this group of men were many friends of the convicted murderers.

The empty *Cyclops* picked up her prisoners and passengers, and then moved to the loading docks. Here her holds were filled with manganese ore. Manganese is added to steel and other metals to make them stronger. Naval ships, guns, propellers, and propeller shafts are made of metal containing manganese. Because of the war, it was an important cargo that the *Cyclops* was to carry back to the port of Baltimore.

Manganese ore is much heavier than coal and much more difficult to load correctly. Only one man on board the *Cyclops* had experience loading manganese ore. This man was Lieutenant Forbes. But Forbes was under arrest. So Captain Worley assigned a young officer to supervise the loading. Again and again the huge scoops dumped the ore into the ship's holds. The *Cyclops* sank lower and lower into the water.

Every large ship has a stripe painted along its sides. This is called the *Plimsall* mark. It marks the safe waterline for a loaded ship. If the ship is loaded with just enough cargo, the waterline will be right on the Plimsall mark. However, after taking on 10,800 tons of manganese ore, the *Cyclops'* Plimsall mark was far below the water line. Captain Worley must have known his ship was overloaded, but he ordered it underway.

The *Cyclops* sailed out of the harbor and headed for the port of Bahia. Bahia is north of Rio de Janeiro. But the reports show that the *Cyclops* entered the harbor at Bahia coming *from* the north. Why had the *Cyclops* sailed past the harbor and then turned around?

The *Cyclops* at the pier, fully loaded.

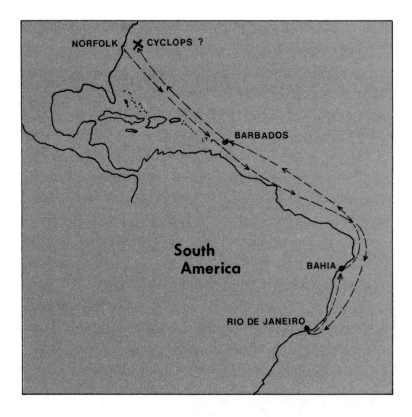

At Bahia, the *Cyclops* picked up another passenger. He was a U.S. diplomat named Alfred Gottschalk. This is interesting because Mr. Gottschalk was, before the war started, very friendly to the German government. He had not approved of the United States getting into the war against Germany.

The *Cyclops*'s orders were to sail directly from Bahia to Baltimore, but she did not follow these orders. Instead she headed east. Time was important. The United States needed her cargo of manganese ore. But on March 3, the heavily-loaded carrier dropped anchor in the harbor of Bridgetown, on the island of Barbados.

Brockholst Livingston was a U.S. diplomat stationed on Barbados. He immediately visited the ship to find out what Worley was doing there. He learned very little during his visit. He did find that the Second-in-Command, Lieutenant Forbes, was still under arrest. Several other crew members and passengers had also been arrested since the ship had left Bahia. Worley claimed that there was a plot against him and his ship. A member of the crew told Livingston that Captain Worley had already hanged one of the men who he thought was plotting against him.

Worley said this story was not true. Besides, his ship needed more food and coal for the long journey home. The records show that the ship had plenty of food and fuel when she had left Brazil just nine days earlier. Still, Worley insisted that 2½ tons of food and 1,500 tons of coal be put on board.

Late the next afternoon, the *Cyclops* left the harbor. Livingston, standing on the docks, saw her clear the entrance. Once clear, she suddenly turned *south* instead of north. In perfectly clear weather, the *Cyclops* steamed across the horizon — and was never seen again!

Two weeks later, the Navy ordered a search for the *Cyclops*. Radio messages went out across the Atlantic. Ships covered every possible route. Islands were searched for signs. No debris was found. No oil slicks were spotted. No survivors were ever heard from.

What had happened to the *Cyclops?* Many theories have been suggested.

One magazine writer suggested that the *Cyclops* was attacked by a giant octopus! He described the an-

USS South Carolina and *USS Cyclops* engaged in experimental "coaling" at sea. Rigging between the ships transferred two 800 lb. bags of coal at one time.

imal as having tentacles the size of trees which it wrapped around the ship. The octopus would have, according to this writer, eaten the crewmen "like berries plucked from a bush." Then the ship and its cargo would have been pulled to the bottom.

A more likely theory is that the convicted men from the *Pittsburgh* took over the ship and sank her. These men then were either lost at sea or managed to reach one of the many islands in the West Indies. If this happened, however, it seems strange that no signs of them or their boats were ever found.

The coal-carrier might have been sunk by a German submarine, of course. Or, perhaps, the German-born Worley and the German-sympathizer Gottschalk turned the ship and its valuable cargo over to the enemy. After World I was over, a search of the German war records showed no evidence that this had happened.

It seems likely that the over-loaded ship simply sank, taking 309 men to the bottom with her. Perhaps

a freak wave or a waterspout hit her and turned her over so quickly that no one was able to send a call for help or launch a life boat. Or perhaps a boiler exploded. However, it is surprising that some debris was never found.

The mystery of the *Cyclops* does not end here. The Newport News shipbuilding company built two other ships identical to the *Cyclops*. These were named the *Nereus* and the *Proteus*. Both ships survived World War I and were later taken out of service. In 1940, both were sold to a Canadian shipping company and made sea worthy.

For the next year, the two ships made regular trips between St. Thomas Island and Norfolk, Virginia. They made the trip about twice a month, carrying loads of aluminum ore bauxite. In late 1941 both ships left St. Thomas in clear weather and calm seas. Like the *Cyclops*, neither was ever heard from again.

The *Nereus* and the *Proteus* (shown here), built like the *Cyclops,* disappeared at sea and were never seen again.

Rescue from the Sea

The Baron Raoul de Reaudéan had finally realized a lifelong dream. He had spent all of his adult life at sea. Now he was, at last, in command of the world's most luxurious passenger liner, the *Ile de France*. The ship's regular commander had suddenly taken "vacation leave." The Baron had been given the ship at the last moment. The rumor was that the captain was ill and wanted to retire. The Baron hoped that he would be given permanent command of the ship, even though he, too, was nearing retirement age.

"What a great way to end a career," he often thought.

The *Ile de France* had been built shortly after World War I. At that time, passenger ships were built for the comfort of their customers. Everything about the ship showed the money and care that had been

She turned over on her right side and slowly sank into the sea.

spent on her. After World War II had ended, she had been completely refitted. Modern equipment had been added to her without destroying her beauty and comfort.

The Baron's trip to New York had been an easy one. The ship had run through a little fog and had arrived a few hours behind schedule. The captain's superiors in the French Line's New York office had warned him about being late. "Our passengers expect to travel in absolute comfort," he had been told. "But they also expect the *Ile de France* to keep her schedule."

The Baron was determined to do just that on the trip back to France. The ship had left New York on time and was steaming for home as rapidly as possible through the fog. Because of the fog, the Baron was on the bridge late on the evening of July 25,

1956. The bridge was crowded with navigation instruments. These included two radar scopes, which he now watched over the shoulder of the operator. With the radar scopes, every ship in the crowded sea lanes around New York harbor could be seen.

The Baron lit a cigarette as he squinted at the radar screens. A green blip showed clearly, an object far to the north of them. The Baron knew this was the Nantucket lightship. The red-hulled Coast Guard ship was permanently anchored some 60 miles south of Nantucket Island. Her job was to warn ships of the hidden shoals nearby. For west-bound ships, it was also the first contact with the United States. It signaled them that New York lay only 200 miles to the west.

Most of the ships that sailed between New York and ports in Europe passed within a few miles of the Nantucket lightship. The area was so crowded with ships that it was often called "The Times Square of the Atlantic" after the busy New York intersection. But instead of cars, busses, and trucks, this intersection brought together hundreds of huge ships.

In 1948 a group called the "Convention for the Safety of Life at Sea," suggested that "traffic lanes" be followed by ships traveling near the lightship. This group suggested that westbound ships use a lane as close to the lightship as possible. Eastbound ships should stay at least ten miles to the south. The *Ile de France,* heading back to Europe, was in the eastbound lane, exactly where she should be.

Another green blip appeared on the radar screen. This one was moving rapidly from the east toward the lightship.

"What ship is that?" the Baron asked the radar operator. The crewman spoke into his telephone to the radio room. Messages flew through the night air.

"That is the *Andrea Doria,* heading for New York."

Baron de Beaudéan knew the *Andrea Doria* well. Everyone who went to sea knew the Italian luxury ship. She was not the largest passenger ship. She weighed only a little over 29,000 tons and was less than 700 feet long. Nor was she the fastest. But she was, without a doubt, the most beautiful passenger ship in the world.

"It looks as though she is going to run over the lightship," the Baron said to the operator. The sight of the two radar blips drawing rapidly together amused him. He realized that the radar was not accurate at this range. The *Andrea Doria* was undoubtedly passing the lightship with a mile or two to spare. He remembered that in 1934 the Greek liner *Olympic* had crashed into the lightship, killing all of the Coast Guardsmen on board. But the *Andrea Doria* had been built only five years ago. She was equipped with all of the navigational equipment she needed to avoid such a disaster, even in a heavy fog.

An hour later, at 11:20, the Baron received an urgent telephone call from the radioman.

"Sir! We have just received an SOS from the *Andrea Doria!*"

The Baron checked his maps. The *Ile de France* was more than 50 miles away from the *Andrea Doria.* It would take them more than two hours to reach her. Being so far away, his ship was not required to respond to the call for help.

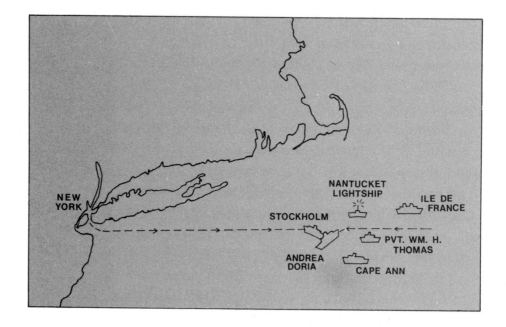

"Are other ships responding?" he asked the radioman.

"Yes, Sir. The *Pvt. William H. Thomas,* the *Cape Ann,* and the *Edward H. Allen* are all within ten to fifteen miles of her and are on their way. The *Laura Maersk* is also responding, but she is two hours away."

The Baron screwed his monocle into his eye and squinted at the books that described these ships. All of them were small. They would not be able to take on many of the 1700 people who were on board the *Andrea Doria.* On the other hand, a ship the size of the *Andrea Doria* could not be in serious trouble. The book told him that she had a double bottom. She also had eleven watertight compartments and would float with any two of them flooded. Even if the *Andrea Doria* were badly damaged, she would float for hours.

She carried 16 lifeboats — enough for 2,000 people. There would be plenty of time to get everyone off.

He lit another cigarette from the one he had been smoking. "I have 900 passengers who expect to arrive in France on time," he thought to himself. "If we are late, I may get in trouble. If we go back all that way for nothing, I may never get command of the *Ile de France.*"

"However," he thought, "the captain of the *Andrea Doria* would not call for help unless the ship is in serious trouble. There are human beings out there, perhaps in the water, needing help."

He ground the cigarette out in an ashtray and ordered his ship to change course. The *Ile de France* made a sweeping curve through the dark water. Her engines throbbed with a deeper note as she was forced to top speed. It was now 11:54, less than 25 minutes after disaster had struck the *Andrea Doria.*

● ● ●　━━　━━　━━　● ● ●

The *Andrea Doria* had passed the Nantucket lightship about a mile to the south, as the Baron had guessed she would. The fog was very heavy. Captain Piero Calamai was on the bridge where he belonged. At 10:45, the man on radar watch called out a warning.

"It's a ship! We can see a ship!"

"What's the distance and bearing?" Captain Calamai asked.

"Seventeen miles. Four degrees off the starboard bow."

As they watched the radar screen, they realized that the green blip was moving in their direction. An eastbound ship was in the westbound lane, and coming rapidly toward them. It looked as if the ship would pass the *Andrea Doria* safely on its starboard side. Captain Calamai ordered his ship to head a little more to port, to give the mysterious ship a little more room. The two ships were now only three and a half miles apart.

The eastbound ship was the Swedish American Line's *Stockholm*. She was the smallest passenger ship in the North Atlantic, only 524 feet long. She weighed only a little more than 12,000 tons. But she regularly carried nearly 600 passengers between Sweden and the United States, using the northern-most routes. She had been especially built for this service. Her bow was pointed and had been reinforced with one-inch-thick steel plates to allow her to follow ice-breakers through the frozen seas around Sweden.

The *Stockholm* was an old ship. Her equipment was out-dated. Her captain, 63-year-old Harry Nordenson, didn't trust his single radar set as much as he did his own feelings for the sea. He had gone to sea at the age of 11 and thought he knew it well. For years, he had taken his ships as close to the Nantucket lightship as possible. He did this whether he was headed east or west. It was stupid, he felt, to swing his ship ten miles to the south to use the eastbound lane. It was a waste of time and fuel. He was being paid to get his passengers to Sweden as quickly and as cheaply as possible.

The *Stockholm* was not in the fog bank that lay to the east of the lightship. Therefore, Captain Norden-

The *Stockholm*, still afloat in spite of her smashed bow, picked up 545 survivors.

son was in his cabin. A young third mate was on the bridge and in command of the passenger liner. At a little after 11:00, he saw the fuzzy blip on the radar screen that was the *Andrea Doria*. It seemed to him that the ship would pass the *Stockholm* on the port side.

The radar showed that the two ships were only four miles apart. The third mate was concerned that the man on watch could not yet see her lights. He did not realize that, just ahead of the speeding *Stockholm*, the night was solid with fog.

The blip on the radar screen showed the distance between the two ships to be only two miles when the man on watch finally spotted the lights of the *Andrea Doria.* "Light on port," he called out. The third mate decided to turn the *Stockholm* to starboard to give the ships a little more room.

As he did so, he realized with horror that the other ship was also turning. At the edge of the fog bank, each ship had turned to avoid the collision. The *Andrea Doria* had turned left and the *Stockholm* had turned right. These turns had brought the *Andrea Doria* directly across the steel-reinforced bow of the *Stockholm.*

Sparks flew high into the dark night. The grinding scream of steel cutting through steel drowned out the screams of the people in the *Andrea Doria*'s starboard cabins. The shock broke one of the Italian ship's bulkheads. Water poured into two of the watertight compartments. As the two ships drifted apart, the *Andrea Doria* listed toward her right side. Water poured through the 50-foot-long gash in her side as A Deck sank beneath the water line. From above, water gushed into the unflooded watertight compartments and they began to fill quickly.

Baron de Beaudéan navigated the *Ile de France* carefully through the fog by use of his radar. From 17 miles away, he spotted four blips on the screen. He could not tell which was the stricken ship. He guided his ship for the nearest blip, intending to work his way from ship to ship until he found the *Andrea Doria.*

Aerial view of the *Andrea Doria*, once considered one of the most beautiful passenger ships in the world.

Eleven of his lifeboats were uncovered and swung over the side. More than 160 of the crew stood ready to lower the lifeboats.

Suddenly, the *Ile de France* broke free of the fog. There, in the moonlight, lay the *Andrea Doria*. The Baron could see that the stricken ship's port-side lifeboats could not be launched. The lifeboats on the starboard side had already been lowered into the water. But the passengers were having to scramble down ropes and nets to get to them.

The Baron carefully brought the *Ile de France* alongside the *Andrea Doria*'s starboard side. This would shelter her and the lifeboats from the ocean's swell. At a distance of about 400 yards, the French ship stopped her engines. Across the water, the Baron could hear the screams, cries, and prayers of the people trapped on the other ship.

"We must let them know we are here," he thought. He ordered all of the ship's lights turned on.

Few people on the *Andrea Doria* had realized that the French liner was nearby. Suddenly, the night blazed with lights. Strings of white bulbs outlined the ship. Every porthole glowed with light. Floodlights were directed upward onto the twin red funnels. The words "ILE DE FRANCE" in huge letters reached across the water toward them.

The bow of the *Stockholm* had smashed through seven decks of the *Andrea Doria*. Forty-six cabins and staterooms, several baggage compartments, two fuel tanks, and a ballast tank had been instantly demolished by the sharp, reinforced steel. Most of the *Andrea Doria*'s passengers were either asleep or were preparing for bed. About 40 of them died instantly in the crash. Hundreds of others were injured.

As the ship rapidly filled with water, it listed more and more. By the hundreds, frantic people tried to make their way up the sloping stairways. Once on deck, they found they had to cling to the railings or crawl on their hands and knees to keep from slipping into the dark water.

Sailors had rushed to their assigned emergency posts. Those who went to the left side of the ship found that they could not launch their lifeboats. The *Andrea Doria* was listing so far to starboard that the boats on the port side would not slide down into the water. With half of the ship's lifeboats useless, there was boat space for only 1,000 of the 1,700 people on board.

On the other side of the ship, the lifeboats were being launched easily. But they swung so far out that the passengers could not climb onto them from the deck. The boats had to be dropped completely into the water. Ropes and nets were thrown over the side of the ships.

One by one, the passengers slid down the ropes or climbed down the nets into the boats. Some jumped from the slanting decks and swam to the boats.

Soon the few lifeboats from the *Andrea Doria* were joined by others. Two motorpowered lifeboats from the *Stockholm* were the first to arrive. Then many boats, manned by sailors from many nations, joined in. In the darkness, six ships stood by to help in the rescue.

On the *Andrea Doria,* a few crewmen panicked and thought only of saving themselves. But most of the crew did heroic acts to save the helpless passengers.

One Italian sailor climbed down a rope with an elderly woman tied to his back. He placed her safely in the lifeboat and then climbed back to the deck. He immediately heaved another frightened woman over his shoulder and again climbed down to the pitching lifeboat. When he was certain she was safe, he quickly climbed back onto the sinking ship and waved the lifeboat away.

Other crewmen stayed in the depths of the ship until the last minute, searching for injured and

trapped people. Dozens and dozens of lives were saved by these brave men.

At about ten the next morning, the stricken *Andrea Doria* gave a sigh and collapsed onto her right side. Water gushed into her funnels. Water spurted from her broken port-side portholes. The beautiful ship had finally died.

Eleven hours after the collision, the bow of the *Andrea Doria* slid under the water. Her twin propellers rose free and she seemed to pause for a moment. Then she plunged rapidly out of sight, leaving only a whirlpool and some debris to mark her grave.

The *Ile de France* was the last ship to arrive on the scene, but she was by far the largest. Her crew picked

up a total of 753 survivors from the *Andrea Doria.* The *Stockholm* was still afloat, in spite of her smashed bow. She took 545 survivors aboard. The *Pvt. William H. Thomas,* the *Cape Ann,* and the *Edward H. Allen* took on about 100 each. Only 46 passengers from the *Andrea Doria* and five crewmen from the *Stockholm* were missing. Almost all of these had been unlucky enough to be sleeping near the point of the collision.

Many people were injured, of course. On board the *Ile de France* doctors worked through the night as the liner sped toward New York. The hospital room was filled with people with broken bones and cuts.

Elsewhere on board, survivors celebrated their rescue. Long tables were set up on the decks. Gallons of coffee and soup, and hundreds of sandwiches were served. Passengers on the French liner donated clothing to the *Andrea Doria*'s passengers. The radio was kept busy with messages carrying news of the disaster.

The *Ile de France* neared New York early the next evening. The Baron de Beaudéan again thought about his passengers and his schedule. He radioed ahead to his superiors in New York, asking that tugs be sent out to meet the ship. He would, he suggested, transfer the survivors to the tugs and head back to France without docking.

"Have you fallen on your head?" the reply came back. "Everyone in New York is waiting for you."

As the *Ile de France* entered the harbor, she was greeted by every ship afloat. Ocean liners, merchant ships, tugs, ferries, motorboats, even small sail boats

This U.S. Coast Guard ship responded to the S.O.S.

came out to meet her. Whistle blasts cut the air. Fire-boats sprayed the ship's sides with streams of water. On the docks lining the harbor, thousands of people cheered the heroic ship and her crew.

Back in France, the Baron received another hero's welcome. He received a decoration from the French Government. But most important to him, in 1957 he was given permanent command of the *Ile de France*.

"The Thresher's a Coffin"

CHAPTER SEVEN

"I'm scared to death," the sailor told his wife. "I have a feeling this will be our last trip."

The machinist's mate was usually a happy-go-lucky fellow. He was a naturally friendly person with a quick smile. Everyone liked him. But today, as he stood on Dock 11 at Portsmouth, New Hampshire, he grimly said goodby to his wife for what he felt would be the last time.

The machinist's mate was not easily frightened. He had been in the Navy for more than 20 years. Many of these years had been spent in submarines. During World War II he had gone into battle on three different subs — the *Sea Dragon*, the *Salmon*, and the *Diodon*. He enjoyed the life on a submarine and usually looked forward to going to sea.

But this trip was different. The sub *Thresher* (SSN-593) had spent the last nine months in dry dock being overhauled. The machinist's mate had worked on the boat during the repair work.

"We hurried too much," he complained to his wife. "We had too many problems from the beginning. We should have taken more time on her. The *Thresher*'s a coffin. Before this week is over, you will be a rich widow."

He kissed his wife and boarded the sleek submarine. At 9:17 the next morning, he and 128 other men were dead. And their coffin was the submarine named *Thresher.*

The first submarine powered by nuclear energy was the *Nautilus.* She was built in 1954. She and thir-

USS Thresher (SSN 593), the first "killer" sub to be put into service.

teen other similar submarines guarded the United States from attack by surface ships.

Then came the *Polaris*-type submarines. These huge boats were able to launch missiles from underwater. The missiles carried nuclear warheads. With them, the U.S. Navy could, if necessary, destroy missile sites in almost any country in the world.

The Russians, once they learned how to control nuclear energy, began to build their own nuclear submarines. The United States decided that a submarine was needed that could find and destroy other submarines. Such subs were to be known as "killer subs."

The *Thresher* was the first killer sub to be put into service. She took her name from the long-tailed Thresher shark. This shark is supposed to capture its prey by thrashing its tail violently from side to side as it swims through a school of fish. It then turns around and eats the injured fish.

The U.S. Navy's first atomic-powered submarine, *USS Nautilus* (SSN 571), on its initial sea trials.

The *Thresher* had cost $45 million to build, and the Navy felt she was worth every penny. She proved, in many ways, to be the best submarine in the world. She could dive deeper than any other sub. She was faster underwater than even the fastest surface ship. She could slip through the water without making even the slightest sound. And she could "hear" other submarines long before they knew she was anywhere around. Her navigation equipment and nuclear power allowed her to travel to any part of any ocean without ever surfacing.

This was the most comfortable submarine ever built. The boat was more than 275 feet long. Her regular crew of 12 officers and 96 enlisted men had more room than most submariners did. Near the middle of the boat, where most of the men lived and worked, the *Thresher* was big enough to be divided into four levels.

Inside a closed, submerged submarine, a lot of different smells come from the machinery, the chemicals, smoking, and cooking activities. But the air inside the *Thresher* was kept cleaner than the air of most large cities. Fresh oxygen was constantly pumped into the air. The temperature was kept within two degrees of 70° F. And the humidity was held at a constant and comfortable 50 percent.

Her living and working quarters had been designed by an interior decorator. The walls were a pleasant shade of brown and the ceilings were white. Matching formica covered the table tops and patterned brown-and-white linoleum covered the decks. These pleasing decorations caused some problems, however. The ceiling and wall panels often had to be removed to get to the pipes and wires behind them. This, of course, made repairs more difficult and time consuming.

Music was piped throughout the submarine for the crew's enjoyment. A different movie was shown every evening. The food was good and was available anytime a crew member was hungry.

There had been problems with the *Thresher*, of course. No one had ever built a submarine like her before, and many small mistakes had been made. After a year of service, the boat had been ordered back to Portsmouth for overhaul.

The Navy wanted the valuable boat back in service as quickly as possible. The repair work on her was pushed hard. Within nine months, the *Thresher* was ready for duty again. At least, everyone thought she was. Everyone, that is, except the machinist's mate whose wife tearfully stood on Dock 11 and watched the submarine pull slowly away.

At 6:15 a.m., April 1, 1963, the *Thresher*'s Engineering Officer reported that the nuclear power unit was producing heat. This heat was used to change water to steam. The steam then turned huge turbine engines. These produced the 18,000 horsepower that was used to push the submarine through the water.

The cruise was to last only two days. Its purpose was to test the repairs that had been made on the submarine. In addition to the boat's regular crew, 20 observers were on board. Most of them were civilians who had worked on the sub's overhaul. They were there to check on the work that had been done. They wore different colored hard hats and were constantly making notes on clipboards they each carried.

By 7:15, the *Thresher* was producing a full head of steam. The lines were cast off, and she left the harbor. She ran on the surface for a while, testing the navigation and communication systems. Everything seemed to work well. Out at sea, she met the *USS Skylark*.

The *Skylark* was a 25-year-old submarine-rescue ship. Her assignment was to stay in close contact with the *Thresher* during the sub's sea trials. The *Skylark* carried an old McCann rescue chamber. It could be used to take men from a damaged submarine at a depth of 850 feet or less. If the *Thresher* had trouble in water deeper than this, everyone knew the *Skylark* would be of no help.

A cutaway drawing showing the inside of the McCann rescue chamber.

For the rest of the day, the *Thresher* ran tests in water above the Continental Shelf. That meant that the bottom was 600 feet or less below the sea's surface. The sub made several dives to 400 feet without problem. She also tried several runs on the surface at top speed. The boat seemed to be working well.

There was one major problem with the design of the *Thresher*. Once submerged, it was necessary to use the engines to drive the submarine to the surface. A submarine will sink when seawater is allowed to enter its tanks. The water-filled sub becomes more dense than the water surrounding it. This seawater must be blown out of the tanks by compressed air. When the tanks are empty, older submarines bob quickly to the surface. But the *Thresher* would not. The Captain found it necessary to push the boat upward through the water under power, even when the tanks were empty.

At 7:45 the next morning, the *Thresher* met the *Skylark*. Together they traveled to a point just off the Continental Shelf. Here the water was more than a mile deep.

"Rig for deep submergence!" the Captain commanded.

The *Thresher*'s powerful engines whined and drove the huge boat under the waves. Deeper and deeper she went. The men on the *Skylark* listened carefully to the radio.

At 400 feet, the *Thresher* reported that everything was going well. At 600 feet, the sub seemed to be completely watertight. By 9:00 o'clock, the *Thresher* had reached a depth of nearly 1,000 feet below the surface. The water around her pushed against every square inch of the steel hull with a pressure of nearly 500 pounds! This was as deep as the submarine had ever been before.

Because of the distance between them, the radio communication between the *Skylark* and the *Thresher* had become very poor. It was very difficult for the men on the *Skylark* to understand what was being reported by the men below.

At 9:13 a faint message came through.

"Experiencing minor difficulty . . ."

The *Thresher* was in trouble. Then, at 9:17, another message came through.

"We are exceeding test depth . . ."

The men on the *Skylark* heard the sound of rushing air that cut off the rest of the message. Then sounds that may have been an explosion. Nothing was heard from the *Thresher* again.

No one knows exactly what happened 1,000 feet below the surface of the Atlantic. But many people who knew the *Thresher* well have made guesses that may be fairly accurate.

A small leak may have developed somewhere on the sub. The water, under tremendous pressure, may have caused an important electrical system to short out. This may have caused the nuclear reactor to shut down temporarily, leaving the submarine running on only electric motors. These were not strong enough to drive the large submarine upward. Once the reactors began to cool, it would take several minutes before the turbines got enough steam to give the boat full power.

The accident probably happened at the sub's lowest diving depth. For some reason, the *Thresher* was apparently unable to hold herself at this depth. As she drifted slowly deeper and deeper, the men inside must have worked frantically to stop the leak, blow the seawater from the ballast tanks, and bring the reactor back to "critical." But it was too late. The deeper she went, the greater the pressure became.

More leaks must have developed. Then, suddenly, the shell of the submarine probably collapsed. As the water pressure reached the diesel fuel aboard, there probably was an explosion that ripped the steel hull into thousands of pieces. Everyone on board must have died instantly.

The *Skylark* reported that she had lost contact with the *Thresher.* All ships in the area were sent to help in the search. No one spoke about "rescue." Everyone knew there was no hope for the men aboard the submarine.

Six hours after the *Thresher*'s last message, an oil slick and a few bits of plastic were found floating on the ocean's surface. During the next two days, a collection of pieces of cork, two rubber gloves, and more bits of plastic were taken from the sea by the search vessels. It could not be proven that this debris came from the missing submarine, but everyone assumed that it did.

The Navy wanted to know what had happened to the *Thresher,* or at least be certain that she had actually sunk. But the Navy had no way of reaching the wreck, lying more than a mile and a half below the surface. Scientists from all over the United States were called in to help in the search. These men and women brought with them some of the equipment they used to study the bottom of the ocean. One of these pieces of equipment was the famous *Trieste.*

In 1960, the *Trieste* had carried two scientists into the deepest trench in the ocean floor — more than *seven miles* below sea level! The research vessel was the invention of a Swiss scientist named Auguste Piccard. Before he became interested in studying the

oceans, Piccard had built balloons used to study the top of the earth's atmosphere. The *Trieste* looked something like a huge gas-filled balloon. The crew rode in a ball that hung down under a blimp-shaped hull. But this hull was not filled with helium. Instead, compartments in the *Trieste* were filled with gasoline, which is less dense than water.

Several scientific instruments, including cameras, were used to search the ocean's floor. These found a number of mounds that might have been debris from the *Thresher*. The *Trieste*'s job was to search each of these mounds to see if any of them contained parts of the missing submarine.

The Bathyscaph *Trieste,* built to study the bottom of the ocean, was used in the search for the *Thresher.*

Again and again the *Trieste* dove to the bottom. There is, of course, no natural light deep under the sea. So a huge, battery-powered searchlight was used. Every inch of the ocean's floor near where the *Thresher* was thought to have landed was carefully searched.

It was slow, discouraging, dangerous work. The *Trieste* had not been built for this type of work. She had never before made more than one dive without being taken back to port for inspection and repairs. But there was no other ship able to dive so deep and return to the surface.

On July 1, the *Trieste* was making its fifth dive to the bottom. Then suddenly, something glowing yellow was seen lying in the mud. The crew inside the *Trieste* edged the craft closer. The yellow blob looked like a shoe cover, the kind worn by people who work near the nuclear reactor of a submarine. Bits of paper and a few chips of paint were also scattered around the shoe cover. A trail of debris led off into the darkness.

At last! Here was something to work with! The crew of the *Trieste* felt certain that at the end of the string of debris lay the wreck of the *Thresher*. The *Trieste* moved forward, inch by inch, following the trail. The search was nearly over.

But then the light began to fade. The batteries that powered the searchlight were beginning to run down! The *Trieste* had to give up the search and return to the surface.

The pressure of the deep dives had damaged the *Trieste* so badly that she had to be returned to Boston for repairs. While she was there, she was fitted with a mechanical arm that would allow her to gather up some of the debris she had found. It was nearly eight weeks later before the *Trieste* was back diving at the disaster site.

Trieste II, a later model, at Boston, Massachusetts, prior to being towed out to sea.

Debris photographed by the *Trieste* on the ocean floor—an external portion of a sonar dome used exclusively in Thresher-class submarines.

It was not easy to find the exact spot where she had been before. On the third dive, on August 28, the men inside the *Trieste* again spotted the yellow shoe cover. Their batteries were strong this time, and they moved ahead quickly. Every mound in the silt covering the ocean bottom was carefully checked.

Within a few minutes they were surrounded by what they described as ''a junkyard.'' Towering chunks of metal lay everywhere. Twisted cable curled

across the ocean floor. Tiny pieces of plastic and rubber littered everything they saw. A twisted, broken, brass pipe lay directly in front of them. The mechanical arm moved out and grasped the pipe tightly. The *Trieste* rose carefully to the surface.

On the deck of the surface ship, the two-yard-long pipe was studied carefully. On its side was some writing that said, "593 Boat." The *Thresher* had been found!

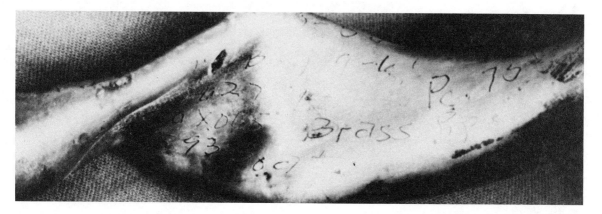

Twisted brass pipe from the *Thresher* recovered from the ocean floor by means of a mechanical arm on the *Trieste*.

What Happened to the Yarmouth Castle?

CHAPTER EIGHT

News of the disaster aboard the cruise ship *Yarmouth Castle* reached Nassau long before the rescue ships. Friends and relatives of the passengers and crew of the cruise ship, plus hundreds of curious onlookers, gathered at the harbor. They crowded onto the Prince George docks, on Bay Street, near the straw market. This was where the *Yarmouth Castle* would have landed if the terrible tragedy had not struck her the night before.

At about three in the afternoon, instead of the familiar white *Yarmouth Castle,* it was the Finnish merchant ship *Finnpulp* and the cruise ship *Bahama Star* that eased up to the dock. The rails of both ships were lined with people. Most of them stared at the Bay Street pier and the crowd of people who stood there

The Evangeline, before she was refitted, repainted and renamed the *Yarmouth Castle*.

waiting for them. No one cheered. No one waved. No one smiled.

The survivors who were on stretchers left the rescue ships first. Crude bandages covered their burns. Then the less-seriously injured made their way down the gangplanks. Most of them were dressed in pajamas and robes. Some were wrapped in blankets. Many were weeping as they left the rescue ships.

The *Finnpulp* brought 93 survivors of the *Yarmouth Castle* to Nassau. The *Bahama Star* carried another 366. The badly injured were rushed to the nearby hospital as soon as the ships berthed. Other survivors of the *Yarmouth Castle* were met by local residents and hurried off to the safety and comfort of a home. The officers of the sunken ship brushed off the reporters in the crowd. They hurried to the shipping line's offices to tell their stories in private.

Many of the *Yarmouth Castle's* survivors and their rescuers were uninjured. As the shock of the disaster began to wear off, many of them were willing to talk about their adventure to anyone who would listen. And the dock was filled with people who wanted to know what had happened to the *Yarmouth Castle* that November night in 1965.

"We left Miami yesterday evening, around five o'clock," one man mumbled to a reporter. "I don't know how many people were on board."

"There were about 375 passengers," one of the crewmen said, "and 176 in the crew."

Slowly the reporters put together the story of the disaster that had struck the *Yarmouth Castle*.

Sixty-one of the passengers were elderly people, all members of the North Broward, Florida, Senior Citizens Club. Many of them were not able to get around easily, but the group had decided to take a vacation in the sun of Nassau anyway. They had supposed that the trip would be easier on their older members if they traveled by ship.

Most of the passengers on the *Yarmouth Castle* were headed for vacations in Nassau. Only a few lived on the islands or were going there on business. The *Yarmouth Castle* was a vacation ship now, but she had not always been.

The ship had been built in 1927. For 37 of her 38 years she had carried passengers in different parts of the world with the name *Evangeline* painted on her bow. During World War II, she had been used to

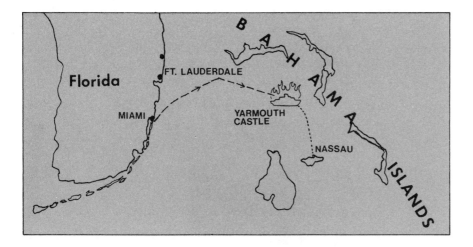

carry troops across the Pacific Ocean and had made many trips without any trouble. She had come through the war without a scratch and many of her crew considered her to be a good-luck ship.

After the war, the *Evangeline* had been taken back to the Atlantic Coast. For the next twenty years, she carried passengers between Boston and Nova Scotia. The crewmen who worked on her during that time claimed that the ship was in good shape and she had a record of dependable service.

"It wasn't her age that caused the trouble last night," one crewman told a reporter. "She was a good-luck ship, right up to the time they changed her name. It's wrong to change the name of a ship," he insisted.

The reporters found that the *Evangeline* had been sold nearly a year before the disaster. The new owners had put the ship into drydock for repairs, and while she was there, the name *Evangeline* had been removed. The new name *Yarmouth Castle* had been painted on.

A lot of other painting was done on the ship while she was in drydock. The old ship had a lot of wood on her. The decks were wooden. Almost every room — every stateroom, the dining rooms, the game room — were paneled with wood. All this wood, along with most of the metal parts of the ship, had been painted over and over again. One passenger insisted that there ". . . must have been 20 coats of paint on everything."

The idea that changing the name of a ship is bad luck is one of the many superstitions of the sea. But in the case of the *Yarmouth Castle,* many claimed it was true. From the time she left the drydock, with her shiny coat of new paint and her new name, she ran into trouble. And bad luck seemed to follow her from the time she reached Florida until that terrible night in 1965.

The run from Miami to Nassau was an easy, overnight cruise. But the *Yarmouth Castle* never seemed to make the trip without problems of some kind. Several times, she broke her moorings while tied up in one harbor or the other. She always seemed to arrive late, for one reason or other. On one cruise, her fresh water system broke down. She even ran into a whale once!

The last cruise of the *Yarmouth Castle* had begun pleasantly the night of November 12. A few of the survivors complained that the ship began to pitch and roll as soon as they left the harbor at Miami. Some of the seasick passengers and many of the older people went to bed early. But the rest had a fun-filled evening. They danced to the music of a live band. There were several kinds of card games going on. Motion pictures of horse racing allowed those who wanted to the chance to gamble. And the floor show began right on schedule, a half hour before midnight.

An hour and a half later, the show was over and most of the passengers had gone to bed. A few people sat quietly in the lounge, playing cards and talking. The stewards were hurrying to finish cleaning up, so they, too, could get some sleep.

The sailor who had the security watch had finished his rounds and was on his way back to the bridge. It was a beautiful night. He stopped for a moment to look at the stars. It was then that he smelled smoke.

"The cook's burning something again," he said to himself as he headed for the galley. But he found the stove cold and clean. He checked a few of the storerooms nearby. The smell of smoke had become stronger. He called the bridge and suggested that the Captain be called.

The Captain, however, was already searching for the fire. The smell of smoke had made its way through the ventilator system to the engine room and had already been reported to the bridge. Several of the passengers from the lounge and members of the night cleaning crew had also smelled the smoke and were busy searching for the fire.

They quickly found that smoke was pouring from under the door of a rest room just off the main lounge. Captain Byron Voutsinas called his crew to the door and pulled it open. Billows of smoke poured from the room, but when the men entered with their fire extinguishers, they found no flames.

"The smoke is coming from below," Captain

Voutsinas guessed. "Let's try the next deck down."

Immediately below the rest room was Room 610. It was a small room, without windows, and very close to the galley. It had been discovered a long time ago that Room 610 was too hot for passengers. So, when the *Yarmouth Castle* had been remodeled, 610 had been turned into a store room. Into it, the crew had pushed anything they wanted to get out of sight. The room was piled high with broken furniture, torn mattresses, and other junk. Because Room 610 was not to be used by passengers, it had not been fitted with sprinkler system outlets.

The crew could feel the heat of the fire through the door of Room 610. When they pushed the door open, flames burst out onto the deck.

The men were, of course, ready with their fire extinguishers. But the heat of the flames kept them back. They tried using the extinguishers from where they were, but the flames still roared, filling the room.

"Get the firehose," the Captain ordered.

The nearest firehose was on a spool only a few yards down the deck. One seaman grabbed its brass nozzle and pulled. A few feet of hose rolled from the spool and then fell to the deck. The hose had been cut and was useless!

The *Yarmouth Castle* shown at the Prince George Wharf, Nassau, about four months before the fatal fire.

The fire broke out of Room 610. The wooden decorations of the deck caught on fire and the flames spread rapidly. The fire fed on the old, painted wood of a stairway and, fed by heated air that rushed up the opening, flashed upward. At the top of the stairs was the wooden bridge and radio shack. Both of these burst into flames and the men inside ran for their lives. The Captain stood in helpless horror. The button that set off the alarm to warn the passengers and crew of danger was in the now-burning rooms.

A woman passenger and her mother shared a stateroom near Room 610. They were awakened by the running and shouting of the men outside. They opened their door and found the passageway full of smoke. They held their breaths and ran to the deck.

Deeper within the ship, few people realized anything was wrong. One couple smelled smoke. The man got out of bed and opened the door. A sailor came by and told him that the fire was out. "Everything is all right," he said. "Go back to bed."

A few minutes later, the couple heard screaming outside their door. This time they both went into the hall. A woman ran past them. "I can't find my baby," she screamed. By this time, the hall was filling with smoke. The couple gathered up their robes and made their way quickly to the deck.

On the deck below, an elderly couple slept through the first noises of the fire. By the time they realized anything was wrong, the hallway outside their cabin was full of black, acrid smoke. They got down on their hands and knees and began to crawl. Blinded by the smoke, they turned a corner and were met by a wall of fire. They quickly turned around and crawled the other way. The man felt certain they were lost in the maze of passageways, but after what seemed like a long time, they found a stairway that led upward onto the deck.

Three elderly sisters in a nearby cabin didn't realize there was trouble until the fire reached their cabin. Tears rolled down the face of one of the ladies as she later recalled the horror. "The door was on fire. We knew we couldn't get out. Just then, the glass in the porthole was smashed. One of the crewmen stuck his head inside and told us to come on. He was hanging by his knees from the railing on the deck above. But he reached in and grabbed me by the arm. Before I knew it, he had pulled me out the window and up onto the deck.

"He hung back down over the side of the ship and pulled my older sister out. I could hear Ellen — she's my younger sister — screaming inside. The sailor swung down again and reached through the porthole, trying to find her. But the flames rushed out and burned him. We knew it was too late!"

With the ship's bridge and radio shack on fire, there was no way to send a radio call for help. Fortunately, the *Finnpulp* was only about six miles away. The fire was sighted from the *Finnpulp* almost as soon as it broke out. After sending an SOS, she headed for the burning ship.

The *Bahama Star* saw the fire too. She had followed the *Yarmouth Castle* out of Miami and was trying to beat her to Nassau so she could unload her passengers first. A crewman on the *Star* was watching the ship on the radar. He saw her suddenly turn and stop. Soon afterwards those awake on the *Star* saw the flames. An alarm was sounded and the *Star's* lifeboats were made ready.

The *Yarmouth Castle* was able to get four boats into the water. The other ten were never used. Some of the survivors claimed that the pulleys stuck when the crew tried to lower these boats into the water. All the ropes had been painted to make them look new and pretty!

The Captain and several sailors were in the first boat launched. Later the Captain said he was going for help. It is true that he did return to the *Yarmouth Castle* once he had asked the *Finnpulp* to send an SOS. Some of the sailors on the *Finnpulp* claimed the boat returned to the flaming cruise ship only after being ordered to do so by the *Finn pulp's* captain.

Each of the survivors had a story to tell. One of the young women who had been aboard reported, "We kept moving around, trying to get away from the flames. Mother and I finally went to the back of the boat, behind the swimming pool.

"Someone on the *Bahama Star* yelled at us to jump and her boats would pick us up. But the members of our crew told us the water was full of sharks and to wait there for a lifeboat. We did as the crew said, but the wait seemed like days instead of a few minutes."

"There wasn't any panic, though," another woman passenger commented. "The men passengers and the crew helped the women and children off first. The crew did a fine job."

"I got out through a porthole," still another passenger said. "A sailor lifted me through. I didn't have a lifejacket. I slid down a rope until I was nearly to the water. There weren't any boats around, and I just hung there. Fire was falling all around me. It was getting unbearably hot. Just then, a motorboat from the *Finnpulp* came by and picked me up.

"I guess I was among the last group to leave the ship. As we pulled away, one of the crewmen told us to be quiet and listen. The night was full of strange, moaning sounds. 'She's dying,' the sailor told us."

A sailor spoke quietly as he described the death of the ship. "Metal turned red and softened and fell into the water. The *Castle* listed more and more. She was ablaze from stem to stern. At dawn, she rolled slowly onto her port side and went down stern first in a cloud of steam.

"It was a very sad sight to see," he said softly.

Fire swept through the ship early in the morning. This photograph was taken by a passenger aboard the rescue ship *Bahama Star*.

Acknowledgements

Photographs in this book are reproduced through the courtesy of the
following:

The Mariners Museum   pages 3, 54, 57, 62-63

Todd Anderson   page 5

© Whaling Film Corporation of New Bedford, Mass.   page 7

The Library of Congress   page 13

The National Maritime Museum, London   pages 16-17, 24-25

The National Army Museum, England   page 23

from *Wreck and Sinking of the Titanic* by Henry Neil, Homewood Press,
    Chicago, © 1912 (Chapin Collection)   page 26-27

The Bettmann Archives   pages 34-35, 104-105

U. S. Naval Photographic Center   pages 43, 46-47, 60-61, 65, 71,
    88-89, 90, 93, 94, 98-99, 100-101, 102

National Archives   pages 44-45, 49, 51, 55, 80-81

Virginia State Library   page 67

U. S. Naval Photographic Center, courtesy of Mr. Earle F. Brookins
    page 70

U. S. Coast Guard, First Coast Guard District, Boston, Massachusetts
    pages 72-73, 84-85, 87

Boston Herald-American   page 79

The Daily Press, Newport News, Virginia   page 103

Alexander C. Brown, taken 6/25/65, at Prince George Wharf, Nassau
    page 110

Wide World Photos. By John Masterson   page 115

Maps drawn by Steve Daniels

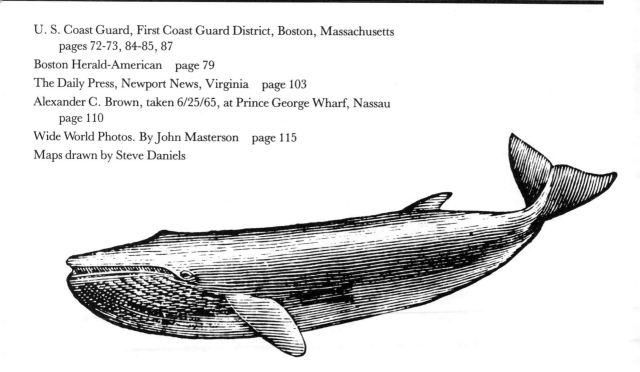

Index